STUDY GUIDE TO ACCOMPANY

Essentials of Psychology in Action

Karen Huffman
Palomar College

Mark Vernoy
Palomar College

Judith Vernoy

Prepared by
Benjamin Wallace
Cleveland State University

JOHN WILEY & SONS, INC.
New York   Chichester   Brisbane   Toronto   Singapore

CONTENTS

HOW TO USE YOUR STUDY GUIDE

First, congratulations on having decided to use <u>Studying Essential Of Psychology In Action: A Study Guide</u> with your textbook, <u>Essential Of Psychology In Action</u> by Huffman, Vernoy, and Vernoy. Hopefully, you are using this study guide to help you achieve the highest grade possible in this, your first psychology course. Although using this study guide does not guarantee that you will earn an "A", the study guide will help you learn the most important material contained in your textbook.

Before using this study guide, however, it is important that you read each assigned chapter and underline or highlight those parts that you believe are the most important. At this point, if you use the study guide properly, it begins to become your friend.

After you have underlined what you consider to be the most important material in a chapter, turn to the corresponding chapter in your study guide. For example, after you have read and highlighted the material in Chapter 1, turn to Chapter 1 in your study guide. You will notice that each chapter in the study guide is divided into eight sections: <u>Chapter Outline</u>, <u>Learning Objectives</u>, <u>Key Terms</u>, <u>Fill-In Exercises</u>, <u>Application</u>, <u>Critical Thinking Exercise</u>, <u>Sample Test Questions</u>, and <u>Answers</u>.

The <u>Chapter</u> <u>Outline</u> is a broad overview of the general chapter contents. You will note that space has been provided to the right of each section of the outline. This is intended for you to write any notes to yourself that come to mind as you examine the outline. Some of these notes may be useful in studying for tests and for testing your knowledge in subsequent sections of the study guide.

After your review of the outline, proceed to the <u>Learning</u> <u>Objectives</u> section. This section states specifically what you should know when you finish studying the chapter. As you proceed through this section, if you encounter a problem and do not know the answer to a learning objective, return to your textbook to find additional information that will enable you to respond to the specific item. Once you have mastered the <u>Learning</u> <u>Objectives</u>, you are ready to proceed to the next section of the study guide, <u>Key</u> <u>Terms</u>.

The <u>Key</u> <u>Terms</u> section is basically a list of terms you need to know. These are the most important terms contained in the chapter of your textbook. As a result, you can expect to see many of these terms used by the instructor in lectures. You can also expect to find many or most of these on your exam. Thus, you should define each of these <u>Key</u> <u>Terms</u> in the space provided. If you do not know the definition of a term or concept, refer back to the section in your textbook chapter where all of the <u>Key</u> <u>Terms</u> are defined for you.

When you have become familiar with the <u>Key</u> <u>Terms</u>, you are ready to tackle the next section, the <u>Fill-In</u> <u>Exercises</u>. This portion is prepared with important words or phrases missing. These omissions are intentional so that you may fill in each blank. Therefore, after you have read and highlighted the material in a chapter, examined the <u>Chapter</u> <u>Outline</u>, responded to the <u>Learning</u> <u>Objectives</u>, and defined the <u>Key</u> <u>Terms</u>, you can proceed to fill in each blank with an appropriate answer. The appropriate responses to the blanks are found at the end of the study guide chapter. If your answer is not the same as or similar to the one given and if you do not know why you missed the item, turn to the appropriate place in your textbook chapter and review this section before you continue in your study guide.

The next section, <u>Application</u>, involves your ability to respond to questions that test your skill in applying the knowledge acquired from the various chapters. Answer these questions as best as you can. If you need help, you can turn to the specific section of your textbook that discusses the various topic(s).

The <u>Critical</u> <u>Thinking</u> <u>Exercise</u> is similar to that contained in each chapter of your textbook. This exercise in the Study

Guide is shorter and is specifically designed to help you focus
on an affective, a cognitive, or a behavioral critical thinking
skill. Respond to this exercise as best as you can. If you run
into difficulties, you may wish to discuss this exercise with
classmates or you may simply review that section of the textbook
chapter that dealt with the issue. By doing these critical
thinking exercises, you will get a good feel for your knowledge
of a specific area covered by the chapter.

After completing the previously described sections of each
chapter of the study guide, you are ready to be tested for
overall knowledge retention in the format you will likely
encounter on your exams. This is the purpose of the Sample Test
Questions. This section contains a number of multiple-choice
questions that relate directly to the material you have just
studied. Proceed to answer the questions by circling your
response. After doing so for each of the questions, turn to the
end of the study guide chapter where you will find the correct
answers.

In detailing for you how to study for this class, I
recognize that your time is limited and that you may not want (or
need) to write your responses to all sections or do all the
activities in each chapter. I also recognize that students vary
in their individual needs for study aids and that some students

find some chapters more difficult than others. As a result, you may pick the elements that are most useful to your individual needs from the variety of aids provided for each chapter.

If you proceed in the manner that I have detailed, you will improve your chances of earning a higher grade. However, do not take shortcuts. For example, some students mistakenly believe they can use the study guide to pass the course and will not have to read the textbook or pay attention to the instructor's lectures. This belief might prove to be a serious mistake. Also, for studying to be most effective, you must space your study times. You cannot accomplish on the night before the exam all the studying that has been suggested--there is just too much to be learned. In Chapter 6 of your textbook, you will note that cramming or massed learning is not a good method of study. Space your studying throughout the time period allocated by your instructor for the assigned chapters. This method of study will prove to be more beneficial than cramming because you will retain more information and will remember it longer.

Spaced Learning

Let me give you an example of the use of spaced learning. I will assume that your instructor has assigned four chapters for you to read for your first exam. I will also assume that you have been given four weeks to learn the material from these chapters if your class is taught on a semester system (three weeks if your course is taught on a quarter system). With this being the case, you should space your reading and studying so you complete approximately one chapter per week. Thus, in the first week, you should have read Chapter 1 and have followed the study procedures that I previously mentioned. You should also read and study the notes from the instructor's lectures. In the second week, this should have been accomplished for Chapter 2 and so on. After you have read all four chapters and your lecture notes, you should then review by going to your study guide and rereading the material contained in it, including your responses to the various sections. Again, when problems arise, refer to the appropriate section or sections in your textbook for additional clarifications.

Active Learning

It should also be pointed out that learning is much more effective when you are actively responding to the material than when you are a passive recipient. By discussing information with others, asking questions in the classroom, taking notes during lectures, organizing material you have read into diagrams or summaries, and completing the activities in this study guide, you will be taking an active role in your own education. As you probably have discovered, passive reading or listening to lectures is not enough to do well in most college courses.

Prefixes and Suffixes

Sometimes obstacles are encountered in trying to learn the material from your textbook and your study guide. You may find words that are confusing. After all, psychology is a science and scientific words and expressions are used. However, sometimes words that are unfamiliar to you can be deciphered if you know some of the common prefixes and suffixes associated with the terminology of psychology.

Let me illustrate. The word **psychology** consists of a prefix and a suffix. **Psych** means mind and **ology** means the study of. Thus, if you know these, you can figure out that psychology is the study of the mind. Likewise, other complex terms can be understood by breaking them down into comparable units. For example:

Words Beginning With	General Meaning	Example
pseudo-	false	pseudopsychologists (Chapter 1)
trans-	across	transduction (Chapter 3)
un-	not	unconditioned (Chapter 5)
antero-	front	anterograde (Chapter 6)
pre-	before	preconventional (Chapter 8)

post-	after	postconventional (Chapter 8)
intra-	within	intrapsychic (Chapter 11)
inter-	between	interpersonal (Chapter 14)

Words Ending With	General Meaning	Example
-thesis	something to be proven	hypothesis (Chapter 1)
-graphy	representation	tomography (Chapter 2)
-lepsy	seizure	narcolepsy (Chapter 4)
-morphism	having a specific form	anthropomorphism (Chapter 9)
-stasis	balance	homeostasis (Chapter 9)
-medial	middle	ventromedial (Chapter 9)
-osis	condition	psychosis (Chapter 12)
-genic	producing	psychogenic (Chapter 12)

The list of described prefixes and suffixes is by no means exhaustive. There are many more in your textbook and in your study guide. If you learn the common ones, perhaps with the help of a dictionary, this information should prove very helpful in retaining information. It should also be helpful in figuring out the answer to some questions on your exams!

Use of the SQ4R Method of Study

In addition to the general principles of learning that have been mentioned, researchers have also discovered several specific techniques that are useful in improving your studying efficiency. One of the best-known techniques is called the SQ4R method. The symbols S, Q, R, R, R, and R stand for:

Survey   Before you begin each chapter, you should skim the entire chapter, noting the title, major headings and subheadings, and figure captions. Next read the summary at the end of the chapter. This helps organize the material into a larger unit and will help you to focus your attention during later careful reading.

Question   As you are surveying the material, ask yourself questions about what you are going to read. (What did your instructor say about this topic when it was assigned? What questions do the headings and subheadings suggest?) Questions aid retention because they require active participation on your part and increase personal relevance of the material.

Read   The survey and question procedure provides a natural lead-in to careful reading. While reading the chapter, attempt to answer the questions you generated, as well as paying close attention to all figures, tables, and boldfaced terms. Read in small units from one major heading to the next, remembering the principle of spaced versus massed practice.

Recite   Recite means to go over what you just read by either orally summarizing, making notes, or completing the review questions in the text.

Review   Reviewing is a combination of the total SQ4R formula. Briefly repeat the survey and questioning you did before you began the chapter, skim the summary in the back of the chapter, reread all notes, and check your memory by reciting and quizzing yourself.

wRite   Writing is an important element in learning. By writing a response, you will retain more than simply reciting information.

Although the SQ4R method can be used with any textbook, your <u>Psychology</u> <u>in</u> <u>Action</u> (Third Edition) textbook and this study guide have been carefully organized around this technique. Specific directions for use of the SQ4R in the textbook are explained in the textbook preface. To facilitate the use of this method with your study guide, I have organized each chapter into discrete elements which are directly related to the SQ4R method. The <u>Chapter</u> <u>Outline</u> is provided for "surveying and questioning," the <u>Learning</u> <u>Objectives</u> and the <u>Key</u> <u>Terms</u> are provided for "reciting and writing," the <u>Application</u> and the <u>Critical</u> <u>Thinking</u> <u>Exercises</u> are presented for "reciting." The <u>Fill-In</u> <u>Exercises</u> are for "reviewing and writing" and the <u>Sample</u> <u>Test</u> <u>Questions</u> are for "reviewing."

These are my suggestions for how to achieve the most from your study guide and from the course in which you are enrolled. Do the best that you can and good luck!

Benjamin Wallace
Cleveland State University

CHAPTER 1: INTRODUCING PSYCHOLOGY

OUTLINE   (Survey & Question)

Use this outline when you survey the chapter, and enter your
questions and comments in the space provided.

TOPIC   **NOTES**

I. UNDERSTANDING PSYCHOLOGY

   A. The Goals of Psychology:
       Describe, Explain,
       Predict, and Change

   B. Areas of Psychology:
       A Field of Diversity

   C. Gender and Cultural Diversity:
       Cultural Psychology

   D. Psychology in Your Life:
       Separating Fact from Fiction

2

II. PSYCHOLOGICAL RESEARCH

A. Experimental Research:
   The Study of Cause and Effect

B. Nonexperimental Research
   Techniques: Studying the
   Correlates of Behavior

C. Correlation Versus Experimental
   Methods: Which is Appropriate?

D. Evaluating Research:
   Are the Findings Significant?

E. <u>Critical</u> <u>Thinking</u>: Becoming
   a Better Consumer of Scientific
   Research

III. ETHICS IN PSYCHOLOGY

A. Research Ethics:
   Respecting the Rights
   of Subjects

B. Animals in Research:
    Is It Ethical?

C. Clinical Practice Ethics:
    Respecting the Rights
    of Clients

IV. SCHOOLS OF PSYCHOLOGY

A. Structuralism and Functionalism:
    The Earliest Schools

B. The Psychoanalytic and
    Gestalt Schools:
    European Contributions

C. Behaviorism: The Study of
    Observable Behaviors

D. Humanistic Psychology:
    Emphasizing the Uniqueness
    of the Individual

E. Cognitive Psychology: The
    Return to Thought Processes

4

F. Psychobiology: The Brain
    and Behavior

G. Psychology Today:
    An Eclectic View

LEARNING OBJECTIVES   (<u>R</u>ecite & w<u>R</u>ite)

Upon completion of Chapter 1, you should be able to:

1. Define <u>psychology</u>.

2. List and discuss the goals of psychology. What is the
    difference between basic and applied research?

3. List and describe the different major areas of psychology.

4. Describe cultural psychology and culture's influence on
    behavior. Define <u>culture</u> and <u>ethnocentrism</u>.

5. Understand the difference between psychology and
    pseudopsychology.

6. Explain the difference between experimental and nonexperimental research.

7. Define and give examples of all of the following: <u>hypothesis</u>, <u>independent variable</u>, <u>dependent variable</u>, and <u>experimental controls</u>.

8. Discuss the merits and limitations of nonexperimental research techniques (naturalistic observations, surveys, case studies).

9. Describe a correlation and tell how a positive correlation differs from a negative correlation. Explain how a correlation is useful as a research technique.

10. Discuss research and clinical practice ethics. Discuss the rights of experimental subjects.

11. Discuss the issue of ethics in animal research.

12. Describe why it is often necessary to use animals in psychological research.

13. Describe the beginnings of psychology with Wundt and the structuralist school.

6

14. Discuss the similarities and differences between the major schools of psychology (structuralist, functionalist, psychoanalytic, Gestalt, behaviorism, humanistic psychology, cognitive psychology, and psychobiology).

15. Explain what is meant by the term eclectic.

KEY TERMS　　(Recite and wRite)

Upon completion of Chapter 1, you should be able to define the following terms.

Applied Research: _____

_____

Basic Research: _____

_____

Behavior: _____

_____

Behaviorism: _____

_____

Case Study: _____

_____

Cognitive Psychology: _____

_____

Control Condition: _____

_____

Correlation: _____

_____

Covert: _____

_____

Culture: _____

_____

Data: _____

_____

Debriefing: _____

_____

Dependent Variable: _____

_____

Double-Blind Experiment: _____

_____

Eclectic Approach: _____

_____

Ethnocentrism: _____

_____

Experiment: _____

_____

Experimental Condition: _____

_____

Experimenter Bias: _____

_____

8

Functionalism: _____

_____

Gestalt: _____

_____

Gestalt Psychology: _____

_____

Humanistic Psychology: _____

_____

Hypothesis:_____

_____

Independent Variable: _____

_____

Information Processing Approach: _____

_____

Introspection: _____

_____

Naturalistic Observation: _____

_____

Overt: _____

_____

Placebo: _____

_____

Placebo Effect: _____

_____

Population: _____

_____

Pseudopsychologies: _____

_____

Psychoanalytic Theory: _____

_____

Psychobiology: _____

_____

Psychology: _____

_____

Psychotherapy: _____

_____

Replicate: _____

_____

Research Methodology: _____

_____

Sample: _____

_____

Sample Bias: _____

_____

Statistically Significant: _____

_____

Statistics: _____

_____

Stimulus: _____

_____

Structuralism: _____

_____

Subject: _____

_____

Surveys: _____

_____

Theory: _____

_____

Unconscious: _____

_____

Variables: _____

_____

FILL-IN EXERCISES   (Review & wRite)

Fill in the word or words that best fit in the spaces below.

1. _____ psychologists study the influence of culture and ethnic practice on people's behavior in order determine which behaviors are universal to all human beings and which are specific to individual cultures.

2. The goals of psychology are to _____, _____, _____, and _____ behavior.

3. A _____ is a tentative explanation for behavior.

4. A response of subjects in an experiment is the _____ variable.

5. Subjects in a _____ condition are exposed to a zero level of the independent variable.

6. With the research technique of _____, behavior is studied in its natural state or habitat.

7. _____ are relationships between two variables that are used to predict behaviors.

8. The _____ school of psychology originated the method of introspection to examine thoughts and feelings.

9. Freud's approach to studying unconscious conflicts of the mind is called _____.

10. _____ attempts to explain behavior as complex chemical and biological events within the brain.

APPLICATION   (<u>R</u>ecite)

<u>Situation</u>

You have always wanted to try a new approach to help you study for an exam. While your old method of studying the night before seemed to work fine in high school, it does not seem to work well in college.

<u>Questions</u> <u>to</u> <u>Answer</u>

1. What experiment could you design to test different methods for studying for an exam?

2. What would be your independent variable(s)?

3. What would be your dependent variable?

4. What would be some of the necessary experimental controls in your experiment?

12

CRITICAL THINKING EXERCISE (<u>R</u>ecite)

<u>Applying</u> <u>Abstract</u> <u>Thinking</u> (A Cognitive Skill)

In Chapter 1 of your textbook, you learned research terminology which can be used to evaluate reports from politicians, advertisers, teachers, the news media, and even close friends. The following exercise will allow you to practice using some of those terms to critically evaluate several sources of information by asking you to assess the accuracy and worth of their "reports." Read each "research" report and decide what is the <u>primary</u> problem or research limitation. In the space provided, make one of the following marks:

    CC = The report is misleading because correlational
          data are used to suggest causation.

    CG = The report is inconclusive since there was no
          control group.

    EB = The results of the research were unfairly
          influenced by experimenter bias.

    SB = The results of the research are questionable
          because of sample bias.

_____ 1. You have noticed that whenever it rains, you seem not to do well on exams. As a result, you have started to ask some of your instructors if you can take exams on other days.

_____ 2. A domestic auto manufacturer, concerned with slumping sales, conducts a survey in one of their auto plants to determine how employees feel about purchasing a foreign auto.

_____ 3. At a major league baseball park, it has been noticed that beer and soft-drink sales are high when color advertising is used on the new billboard.

_____ 4. A researcher interested in how the public feels about Hollywood gossip publishes a survey in the <u>National Enquirer</u> and asks readers to mail in their responses.

_____ 5. A scientific report has been published that shows that aspirin can cause excessive perspiring. As a result, you stop taking aspirin.

_____ 6. After not doing well on an exam, you ask others who did equally as poor how they feel about the professor.

SAMPLE TEST QUESTIONS   (Review)

1. Which of the following are the goals of psychology?

    a. describe, manipulate, control, and examine behavior
    b. describe, explain, predict, and change behavior
    c. predict, control, examine, and change behavior
    d. manipulate, control, explain, and change behavior

2. Basic research is conducted to study

    a. basic psychological needs such as hunger, socialization, and the need for praise
    b. theoretical questions that may or may not have real-world applications
    c. the goals of psychology
    d. a specific real-world problem

3. Applied research is conducted to study

    a. how people apply knowledge in an educational setting
    b. theoretical questions that may or may not have real-world applications
    c. the goals of psychology
    d. a specific real-world problem

4. These psychologists are concerned with the behavior of people in group situations.

    a. social psychologists
    b. developmental psychologists
    c. school psychologists
    d. organizational psychologists

14

5. The feeling that one's own cultural group is superior to others and its customs and ways of life are the standards by which other cultures should be judged is referred to as:

   a. discrimination
   b. ethnocentrism
   c. egocentrism
   d. ideocentrism

6. Only the experiment allows one to investigate

   a. relationships
   b. correlations
   c. causation
   d. the goals of psychology

7. An educated guess or a possible explanation for a behavior being studied that is expressed as a prediction or a statement of cause and effect is a(n)

   a. correlation
   b. experiment
   c. hypothesis
   d. theory

8. An experimenter wishes to see if there is a difference between two different types of memory techniques. She teaches one group of subjects technique A and another group technique B. Then she gives each group a list of words to memorize. Two weeks later she tests the subjects to see how many of the words they have remembered. What is the dependent variable in this experiment?

   a. the number of words in the list
   b. the memory techniques
   c. the sex of the experimenter
   d. the number of words remembered

9. What is the independent variable in the experiment described in question 8?

   a. the number of words in the list
   b. the memory techniques
   c. the sex of the experimenter
   d. the number of words remembered

10. When subjects are not exposed to any amount or level of the independent variable, they are members of the

    a. control condition
    b. experimental condition
    c. observation group
    d. out-of-control group

11. The tendency of experimenters to influence the results of their experiment in an expected direction is called

    a. experimenter bias
    b. control bias
    c. observational bias
    d. experimental bias

12. When the experimenter and the subjects are unaware of which subjects are part of the control group and which are part of the experimental group, this is referred to as a

    a. single-blind experiment
    b. double-blind experiment
    c. placebo experiment
    d. variable experiment

13. When researchers systematically observe behavior of animals or humans in their natural state or habitat, they are conducting

    a. an experiment
    b. naturalistic observation
    c. a case study
    d. a survey

14. The man who is generally credited with being the founder of experimental psychology is

    a. Sigmund Freud
    b. Wilhelm Wundt
    c. William James
    d. G. Stanley Hall

15. The school of psychology that sought to study the elements of conscious experience was

    a. functionalism
    b. Gestalt
    c. behaviorism
    d. structuralism

16. William James was the leading force in the _____ school of psychology.

    a. behaviorist
    b. functionalist
    c. structuralist
    d. humanistic

17. Which of the following developed psychoanalytic theory?

    a. Freud
    b. James
    c. Wundt
    d. Watson

18. Gestalt psychology studied

    a. the psyche
    b. the perception of wholes
    c. the elements of perception
    d. stimulus and response

19. Humanistic psychology emphasizes

    a. the psyche
    b. the perception of wholes
    c. that human nature is positive and growth seeking
    d. the inner thinking processes necessary for human interaction

20. The information processing approach is used by

    a. humanistic psychologists
    b. behaviorists
    c. functionalists
    d. cognitive psychologists

ANSWERS

<u>FILL-IN</u> <u>EXERCISES</u>

1. Cultural   2. describe, explain, predict, change
3. hypothesis   4. dependent   5. control   6. naturalistic
observation   7. Correlations   8. structuralist
9. psychoanalysis   10. Psychobiology

<u>CRITICAL</u> <u>THINKING</u> <u>EXERCISE</u>

1. CC 2. SB 3. CG 4. SB 5. CG 6. EB

<u>SAMPLE</u> <u>TEST</u> <u>QUESTIONS</u>

1.	b	11.	a
2.	b	12.	b
3.	d	13.	b
4.	a	14.	b
5.	b	15.	d
6.	c	16.	b
7.	c	17.	a
8.	d	18.	b
9.	b	19.	c
10.	a	20.	d

CHAPTER 2: THE BIOLOGICAL BASES OF BEHAVIOR

OUTLINE   (<u>S</u>urvey & <u>Q</u>uestion)

Use this outline when you survey the chapter, and enter your questions and comments in the space provided.

TOPIC   NOTES

I.   THE NEURON

    A.   Structure of a Neuron:
        Three Basic Parts

    B.   Resting Potential and
        Action Potential: To Transmit
        or Not to Transmit,
        That is the Question

II.   CHEMICAL MESSENGERS

    A.   Nervous System Messengers:
        Neurotransmitters

    B.   Endocrine System Messengers:
        Hormones

III. THE PERIPHERAL NERVOUS SYSTEM

    A. The Somatic Nervous System:
       A Network for Sensory and
       Motor Messages

    B. The Autonomic Nervous System:
       Preparing for Fight or Flight

IV. THE CENTRAL NERVOUS SYSTEM

    A. The Spinal Cord:
       The Link Between the
       Brain and the Body

    B. The Brain: The Body's
       Control Center

    C. <u>Gender</u> <u>and</u> <u>Cultural</u>
       <u>Diversity</u>: Sexual Orientation
       and the Hypothalamus

20

D. <u>Gender</u> <u>and</u> <u>Cultural</u>
    <u>Diversity</u>: Male and Female
    Differences in the Brain

V. STUDYING THE BRAIN

    A. Anatomical Studies:
        From Cadavers to Computers

    B. Lesion Techniques:
        Studying the Brain Through
        Systematic Deactivation

    C. <u>Critical</u> <u>Thinking</u>:
        Understanding Brain Anatomy
        and Function

    D. Electrical Recording:
        Measuring Electrical Changes
        in the Brain

    E. Electrical Stimulation:
        Eliciting Brain Activity

F. Split-Brain Research: Two
Brains Rather Than One

G. CAT, PET, and MRI: Techniques
That Scan the Brain

LEARNING OBJECTIVES   (<u>R</u>ecite & w<u>R</u>ite)

Upon completion of Chapter 2, you should be able to:

1. Draw a neuron and label its parts and the functions of each.

2. Describe a resting potential and an action potential.

3. Explain the purpose of the sodium-potassium pump.

4. Explain how neurotransmitters act to produce action
potentials.

5. Briefly explain how psychoactive drugs affect the synapse.

22

6. Describe the endocrine system and explain its major functions.

7. Explain homeostasis.

8. List the parts of the peripheral nervous system.

9. Describe the function of the somatic nervous system.

10. Describe the general function of the autonomic nervous system, including both the parasympathetic and the sympathetic parts.

11. Identify the CNS, the role of the spinal cord, the different lobes of the brain, and the major functions of each.

12. Locate the subcortical brain areas listed in the text and describe the functions of these areas.

13. Locate the cerebellum and the different parts of the brain stem and list their functions.

14. Describe the relationship between the hypothalamus, gender, and sexual orientation.

15. Describe how male and female brains differ. Discuss the tasks that generally favor women as well as those that generally favor men.

16. Explain how the following types of brain research techniques are used to study the brain: (a) lesion techniques, (b) electrical recording, (c) electrical stimulation, (d) split-brain techniques, and (e) CAT, PET, and MRI.

KEY TERMS (Recite & wRite)

Upon completion of Chapter 2, you should be able to define the following terms.

Action Potential: _____

_____

Afferent: _____

_____

All-or-Nothing Principle: _____

_____

24

Association Areas: _____

_____

Autonomic Nervous System (ANS): _____

_____

Axon: _____

_____

Axon Terminal Buttons: _____

_____

Brain: _____

_____

Brain Stem: _____

_____

Broca's Area: _____

_____

CAT (Computerized Axial Tomography) Scan: _____

_____

Central Nervous System (CNS): _____

_____

Cerebellum: _____

_____

Cerebral Cortex: _____

_____

Corpus Callosum: _____

_____

Dendrites: _____

_____

Dyslexia: _____

_____

Efferent: _____

_____

Electrodes: _____

_____

Electroencephalograph (EEG): _____

_____

Endocrine System: _____

_____

Frontal Lobes: _____

_____

Homeostasis: _____

_____

Hormones: _____

_____

Hypothalamus: _____

_____

Ions: _____

_____

Lesion Technique: _____

_____

26

Limbic System: _____

_____

Medulla: _____

_____

Motor Control Area: _____

_____

MRI (Magnetic Resonance Imaging): _____

_____

Myelin: _____

_____

Nerve: _____

_____

Neurons: _____

_____

Neurotransmitters: _____

_____

Occipital Lobes: _____

_____

Parasympathetic Nervous System: _____

_____

Parietal Lobes: _____

_____

Peripheral Nervous System (PNS): _____

_____

PET (Positron Emission Tomography) Scan: _____

_____

Pons: _____

_____

Projection Areas: _____

_____

Psychoactive Drugs: _____

_____

Reflex Arc: _____

_____

Reflexes: _____

_____

Resting Potential: _____

_____

Reticular Activating System (RAS): _____

_____

Reward Centers: _____

_____

Sodium-Potassium Pump: _____

_____

Soma: _____

_____

Somatic Nervous System: _____

_____

Spinal Cord: _____

_____

Split-Brain: _____

_____

Sympathetic Nervous System: _____

_____

Synapse: _____

_____

Temporal Lobes: _____

_____

Thalamus: _____

_____

Wernicke's Area: _____

_____

FILL-IN EXERCISES (<u>R</u>eview & w<u>R</u>ite)

Fill in the word or words that best fit in the spaces below.

1. The nervous system is broken into two major parts: the
   _____ nervous system, which includes the brain and spinal
   cord, and the _____ nervous system, which includes all the
   nerves entering or exiting the brain or spinal cord.

2. The major parts of the neuron are _____, _____, and
   _____.

3. When an action potential is first initiated, _____
   rushes into the axon and _____ ions move out.

4. There are two basic types of neurotransmitters: _____ transmitters, which cause the receiving cell to be more likely to initiate an action potential, and _____ transmitters, which cause it to be less likely to initiate an action potential.

5. The two major parts of the peripheral nervous system are the _____ nervous system and the _____ nervous system.

6. The part of the autonomic nervous system that is dominant during normal nonstressful times is the _____ nervous system. The part of the autonomic nervous system that is dominant during mental or physical stress is the _____ nervous system.

7. The lobes of the brain that contain the area for motor control and Broca's speech area are the _____ lobes.

8. Research has shown that a particular area of the _____ is twice as large in males as in females.

9. The major brain stem structures are the _____, _____, and _____.

10. The three major techniques used for scanning the brain are _____, _____, and _____.

APPLICATION (<u>R</u>ecite)

<u>Situation</u>

Two students enrolled in a psychology class have just read Chapter 2 in the textbook and are discussing the human brain. After reading the portion on the split-brain, one remarks to the other that we really have two brains, not one. The other responds that this cannot be the case.

<u>Questions to Answer</u>

1. Do we really have two brains?

2. What neurological mechanism might account for someone saying that humans have two brains?

3. If we do have two brains, how are they similar?

4. What differences exist in a two-brain system?

CRITICAL THINKING EXERCISE   (R̲ecite)

<u>Clarifying</u> <u>Terms</u> <u>and</u> <u>Concepts</u>   (A Cognitive Skill)

One of the most important elements of critical thinking is clarity of thought. A clear thinker understands that the simple ability to define a term is not evidence of true understanding. One must be able to extend basic definitions to higher, more complex applications. The clear, critical thinker allows his or her curiosity to roam to the "outer limits." They ask questions such as "What does this mean?" "What would happen if ...?" "What if this were different?" They explore core terms and concepts from several different angles. This type of "free-wheeling" exploration not only improves comprehension of the original terms but also encourages the development of general critical thinking skills.

The following exercise will help to clarify your understanding of brain terminology and function. While so doing, it provides a model for the types of questions one asks that lead to critical thinking. By doing these "diagnoses," you will also be practicing another skill involved in critical thinking: employing inductive logic, or moving from the specific to the general.

<u>The</u> <u>Setting</u>

You are a famous neurosurgeon who specializes in brain damage involving the language system. In each of the following cases, make a "diagnosis" concerning where you believe brain damage has occurred.

Case 1:   A 56-year-old female has suffered a recent stroke. She speaks in a curious manner resembling fluent English but the phrases make no sense. You find that she comprehends your verbal or written instructions perfectly and can even write them down, but cannot repeat them verbally. You quickly diagnose the problem as a lesion in the _____.

Case 2: A mother brings her 7-year-old son to you because he is having serious problems in learning to read. At age 5 his corpus callosum was sectioned in order to prevent epileptic seizures. She points out that he is a very intelligent child and she cannot understand why reading is so difficult for him. You explain that his reading difficulties are probably related to the fact that _____.

Case 3: An intelligent businessman comes to you and explains rather agitatedly that he awakened yesterday morning to find, much to his dismay, that he could no longer read. Your tests determine the following:

1. He is totally blind in the right visual field.
2. He speaks fluently and comprehends speech.
3. He can write with his right hand but cannot read what he has written.
4. He can copy written words but only with his left hand.

You turn to your puzzled assistant and remark that this is indeed a tough one, but you are willing to bet you will find brain damage in at least two areas, which are _____ and _____.

SAMPLE TEST QUESTIONS   (Review)

1. Cells within your body specialized for conducting information are called

   a. dendrites
   b. neurons
   c. axons
   d. nucleotides

2. The three major parts of a neuron are the

   a. glia, dendrites, and myelin
   b. myelin, dendrites, and axon
   c. dendrites, axon, and soma
   d. axon, glia, and myelin

32

3. How fast does the average action potential travel in a myelinated neuron?

   a. 100 meters per second
   b. 300 million meters per second (the speed of light)
   c. 1000 meters per second
   d. 10 meters per second

4. The major ions involved in the resting and action potential are

   a. sodium and hydrogen
   b. hydrogen and potassium
   c. DNA and RNA
   d. potassium and sodium

5. Myelin, the fatty insulation surrounding the axon, serves to

   a. slow down sodium ions
   b. increase the speed of the action potential
   c. increase the speed of the resting potential
   d. slow neural transmission

6. The synapse is the point where

   a. the soma attaches to the dendrite
   b. neurotransmitters are manufactured
   c. information transfers from neuron to neuron
   d. the action potential begins

7. Chemical messengers that are secreted into the synapse by axon terminal buttons are called

   a. ions
   b. neurotransmitters
   c. nucleotides
   d. neurocommunicators

8. The principle whereby an axon either fires an action potential or it does not fire an action potential is called the

   a. sodium-potassium principle
   b. axon terminal principle
   c. shotgun principle
   d. all-or-nothing principle

9. The somatic nervous system includes all incoming _____ nerves and all outgoing _____ nerves.

    a. central, peripheral
    b. afferent, efferent
    c. peripheral, central
    d. efferent, afferent

10. The parasympathetic and sympathetic are the major divisions of the

    a. autonomic nervous system
    b. somatic nervous system
    c. central nervous system
    d. automatic nervous system

11. The parasympathetic nervous system is normally dominant when a person is

    a. stressed
    b. relaxed
    c. frightened
    d. asleep

12. The system of glands that secrete hormones into the bloodstream is called the

    a. lympathic system
    b. hormonal system
    c. endocrine system
    d. reticular activating system

13. The major divisions of the central nervous system are

    a. sympathetic and parasympathetic
    b. somatic and autonomic
    c. gray matter and white matter
    d. brain and spinal cord

14. The frontal, parietal, occipital, and temporal lobes make up the

    a. brain
    b. cerebral cortex
    c. subcortex
    d. brain stem

34

15. If you are accidentally hit on the head and you see flashes
    of light, most likely the blow activated cells in the

    a. frontal lobes
    b. temporal lobes
    c. occipital lobes
    d. parietal lobes

16. The corpus callosum, the thalamus, and the hypothalamus are
    all

    a. subcortical areas
    b. cortical areas
    c. brain stem areas
    d. spinal cord areas

17. Damage to the medulla can lead to

    a. loss of vision
    b. loss of respiration
    c. loss of hearing
    d. loss of smell

18. Split-brain research has indicated that, in most people, the
    left hemisphere is responsible for

    a. musical abilities
    b. spatial abilities
    c. artistic abilities
    d. mathematical abilities

19. The control of voluntary movement is found in the

    a. spinal cord
    b. frontal lobes
    c. subcortex
    d. brain stem

20. The three main brain scans discussed in the text are

    a. CAT, DOG, RAT
    b. PET, CAT, MRI
    c. BW, LEF, SS
    d. KSU, HSU, CSU

ANSWERS

FILL-IN EXERCISES

1. central, peripheral   2. dendrites, soma, axon   3. sodium, potassium   4. excitatory, inhibitory   5. somatic, autonomic 6. parasympathetic, sympathetic   7. frontal   8. hypothalamus 9. pons, medulla, reticular formation   10. CAT, PET, MRI

CRITICAL THINKING EXERCISE

Case 1: Left hemisphere, in the frontal and temporal lobes, probably Broca's area.

Case 2: He had his corpus callosum severed, and his frontal, temporal, and occipital lobes are not integrating information.

Case 3: Left occipital lobe, corpus callosum

SAMPLE TEST QUESTIONS

1.	b	11.	b
2.	c	12.	c
3.	a	13.	d
4.	d	14.	b
5.	b	15.	c
6.	c	16.	a
7.	b	17.	b
8.	d	18.	d
9.	b	19.	b
10.	a	20.	b

CHAPTER 3: SENSATION AND PERCEPTION

OUTLINE   (<u>S</u>urvey & <u>Q</u>uestion)

Use this outline when you survey the chapter, and enter your questions and comments in the space provided.

        TOPIC   **NOTES**

I. EXPERIENCING SENSATIONS

    A. Sensory Thresholds: Testing the Limits and Changes

    B. Sensory Adaptation: Weakening the Response

II. VISION

    A. Light: Electromagnetic Energy

    B. The Eye: The Anatomy of Vision

III. THE OTHER SENSES

    A. Hearing

    B. Smell and Taste

    C. The Body Senses

IV. PERCEPTION

 V. SELECTION

    A. Physiological Factors:
       Biological Influences on
       Selection

    B. Stimulus Factors:
       Environmental Influences
       on Selection

38

C. Psychological Factors:
    Intrapsychic Influences
    on Selection

VI. ORGANIZATION

    A. Form Perception:
        Organizing Stimuli into
        Patterns or Shapes

    B. <u>Gender</u> <u>and</u> <u>Cultural</u>
        <u>Diversity</u>: Are the Gestalt
        Laws Universally True?

    C. Perceptual Constancies:
        Stabilizing a Changing World

    D. Depth Perception:
        Seeing the World as
        Three Dimensional

    E. Color Perception:
        Discriminating Among Hues

VII. INTERPRETATION

    A. Early Life Experiences:
       The Effects of Environmental
       Interaction

    B. Perceptual Expectancy:
       The Effects of Prior
       Experience

    C. Other Influences on
       Interpretation: Personal
       Motivations and Frames of
       Reference

    D. Extrasensory Perception:
       Strange But Not True

    E. <u>Critical Thinking</u>:
       Problems With Believing
       in ESP

LEARNING OBJECTIVES   (Recite & wRite)

Upon completion of Chapter 3, you should be able to:

1. Define <u>sensation</u> and <u>perception</u>. What differentiates these processes?

2. Explain transduction, reduction, and coding in sensory processing.

3. Describe absolute and difference thresholds.

4. Explain the importance of sensory adaptation.

5. Describe the physical properties of light and light waves.

6. Draw a diagram of the eye and label its parts.

7. Explain the functions of the different parts of the eye.

8. Describe the functions of rods and cones.

9. Describe dark and light adaptation.

10. Describe the physical properties of sound and sound waves.

11. Identify the parts of the ear and the function of each.

12. Understand how sound waves are transduced into neural impulses by the structures of the ear.

13. Describe the sense organs of smell and taste and how they function. Identify the location of various taste receptors.

14. List and describe the skin senses.

15. Briefly explain the gate-control theory of pain.

16. Explain how the vestibular senses and the kinesthetic sense provide us with information about our body.

17. Describe the three basic processes of perception: selection, organization, and interpretation.

18. Explain what is meant by feature detectors.

19. Describe habituation.

20. Discuss the research on subliminal perception.

21. List and discuss the Gestalt principles of perceptual organization and their possible universality.

22. Explain size, shape, color, and brightness constancy.

23. List and explain the binocular depth cues.

24. List and explain the monocular depth cues.

25. Discuss how both the trichromatic theory and the opponent-process theory are needed to explain how humans see color.

26. Describe how prior experience, personal motivation, and frames of reference affect the interpretations of what we perceive.

27. Describe and discuss the different types of extrasensory perception.

KEY TERMS   (Recite and wRite)

Upon completion of Chapter 3, you should be able to define the following terms.

Absolute Threshold: _____

_____

Accommodation: _____

_____

Aerial Perspective: _____

_____

Amplitude: _____

_____

Aqueous Humor: _____

_____

44

Audition: _____

_____

Auditory Canal: _____

_____

Auditory Nerve: _____

_____

Blind Spot: _____

_____

Body Senses: _____

_____

Brightness Constancy: _____

_____

Ciliary Muscles: _____

_____

Clairvoyance: _____

_____

Closure: _____

_____

Cochlea: _____

_____

Coding: _____

_____

Color Aftereffects: _____

_____

Color Constancy: _____

_____

Cones: _____

_____

Constancy: _____

_____

Contiguity: _____

_____

Continuity: _____

_____

Convergence: _____

_____

Cornea: _____

_____

Dark Adaptation: _____

_____

Depth Perception: _____

_____

Difference Threshold: _____

_____

Eardrum (Tympanic Membrane): _____

_____

Electromagnetic Spectrum: _____

_____

46

Endorphins: _____

_____

Extrasensory Perception (ESP): _____

_____

Feature Detectors: _____

_____

Figure and Ground: _____

_____

Fovea: _____

_____

Frequency: _____

_____

Gate-Control Theory of Pain: _____

_____

Gestalt: _____

_____

Gustation: _____

_____

Habituation: _____

_____

Hair Cells: _____

_____

Hue: _____

_____

Illusion: _____

_____

Incus: _____

_____

Interposition: _____

_____

Iris: _____

_____

Kinesthesis: _____

_____

Lens: _____

_____

Light Adaptation: _____

_____

Light and Shadow: _____

_____

Linear Perspective: _____

_____

Lock-and-Key Theory: _____

_____

48

Malleus: _____

_____

Motion Parallax: _____

_____

Olfaction: _____

_____

Opponent-Process Theory: _____

_____

Optic Nerve: _____

_____

Oval Window: _____

_____

Papillae: _____

_____

Perception: _____

_____

Pheromones: _____

_____

Photoreceptors: _____

_____

Pitch: _____

_____

Precognition: _____

_____

Proximity: _____

_____

Psychokinesis: _____

_____

Pupil: _____

_____

Receptors: _____

_____

Relative Size: _____

_____

Retina: _____

_____

Retinal Disparity: _____

_____

Reversible Figure: _____

_____

Rods: _____

_____

Sclera: _____

_____

Selective Attention: _____

_____

Semicircular Canals: _____

_____

Sensation: _____

_____

Sensory Adaptation: _____

_____

Shape Constancy: _____

_____

Similarity: _____

_____

Size Constancy: _____

_____

Skin Senses: _____

_____

Sound Waves: _____

_____

Stapes: _____

_____

Stereoscopic Vision: _____

_____

Subliminal: _____

_____

Telepathy: _____

_____

Texture Gradients: _____

_____

Transduction: _____

_____

Trichromatic Theory: _____

_____

Vestibular Sacs: _____

_____

Vestibular Sense: _____

_____

Vitreous Humor: _____

_____

Wavelength: _____

_____

FILL-IN EXERCISES   (Review & wRite)

Fill in the word or words that best fit in the spaces below.

1. The process of receiving, translating, and transmitting
    information from the "outside" to the brain is called
    _____.

2. If a researcher were testing to determine the dimmest light
    a subject could perceive, the researcher would be measuring
    the _____.

3. Light waves entering the eye pass through the outer transparent _____ and the opening called the _____ and are focused by the elastic _____ on the _____ at the back of the eye.

4. _____ result from rapid changes in air pressure caused by vibrating objects.

5. According to the _____ theory, we are able to smell a particular odor because the shape and size of its molecule enable it to fit into a certain type of receptor cell.

6. The three basic processes of perception are: _____, _____, and _____.

7. The principle of _____ is at work when, as your brother walks away from you, you don't perceive him to be shrinking.

8. The two main binocular cues to distance are _____ and _____.

9. The color theory that states that there are three color systems---red, green, and blue---is known as the _____ theory.

10. In ESP research, _____ is the ability to predict the future.

APPLICATION (Recite)

Situation

A man walks to the produce counter of a grocery store to buy some fruits and vegetables. He notices all the different types and colors of apples that are now available. He also notices how nicely the produce clerk has arranged them. After admiring the various types of apples, he decides to purchase the green ones.

Questions to Answer

1. How would the trichromatic theory explain his perception of
    the green apples?

2. How would the opponent-process theory explain his ability to
    see green apples?

3. Are there any cultural factors that might have influenced
    this person's displaying a preference for green apples?

4. What Gestalt organizational principles of perception might
    account for the customer's commenting on how nicely the
    apples were arranged?

CRITICAL THINKING EXERCISE   (<u>R</u>ecite)

<u>Empathizing</u> (An Affective Skill)

In Chapter 3, you read about Helen Keller, an extraordinary woman
who was blind from birth. The following exercise will improve
your ability to empathize a bit with her and other visually-
impaired people you might know. As you have read in the text,
noncritical thinkers view everything and everyone else in
relationship to themselves. They fail to understand or
appreciate another's thoughts, feelings, or behaviors, as
critical thinkers do.

Find a partner to take you on a "blind walk" for at least 20 to
30 minutes. Have the partner blindfold you and guide you on a
walk filled with varied sensory experiences--up a hill, over a
gravel driveway, across a dirt field full of potholes, past a
bakery, through the school cafeteria, next to a rough wall, past
an open freezer door, through a quiet library or the noisy
student union, and so on--and see if you can tell where you are
at any one time. Remind your partner not to give any hints as to
what to expect so that it can be a truly sightless experience for
you.

54

What happened when you were without your sense of sight? Did you
find that you navigated better and could more easily determine
where you were at the end of your walk--did you adapt? Did you
compensate at all for your lack of sight--did you substitute
another sense for your sense of sight? In what ways?

SAMPLE TEST QUESTIONS   (<u>R</u>eview)

1. The process of receiving, transducing, and transmitting
    information from the outside world is called

    a. perception
    b. detection
    c. sensation
    d. integration

2. The process of converting a physical stimulus into a nerve
    impulse is called

    a. reduction
    b. conduction
    c. transduction
    d. neural stimulation

3. The lowest or quietest sound people can hear is their

    a. threshold of excitation
    b. absolute threshold
    c. difference threshold
    d. low point

4. The _____ of light determines its hue, while the
    _____ determines its brightness.

    a. wavelength, amplitude
    b. pitch, wavelength
    c. timbre, amplitude
    d. wavelength, frequency

5. The receptors in the eye responsible for daylight and color
   vision are the _____; the receptors in the eye
   responsible for dim light vision are the _____.

   a. rods, cones
   b. hair cells, cilia
   c. lens, cornea
   d. cones, rods

6. The frequency of a sound wave is sensed as the _____
   of a sound.

   a. pitch
   b. intensity
   c. loudness
   d. height

7. The chemical senses are

   a. taste and touch
   b. taste and smell
   c. vision and audition
   d. touch and smell

8. The sensitive area of the nasal cavity where the smell
   receptors are located is called the nasal

   a. retina
   b. cochlea
   c. papillae
   d. epithelium

9. Which of the following is not a skin sense?

   a. pressure
   b. pain
   c. warmth and cold
   d. balance

10. The sense of balance is called the _____ sense.

    a. auditory
    b. gustatory
    c. kinesthetic
    d. vestibular

56

11. The process of selecting, organizing, and interpreting
    sensory data into a usable mental representation of the
    world is the definition of

    a. sensation
    b. perception
    c. transduction
    d. adaptation

12. Subliminal messages, those messages presented below
    threshold, can affect behavior in which of the following
    ways?

    a. they can help you learn while asleep
    b. they can cause you to change your behavior to comply
        with the message
    c. both a and b
    d. subliminal messages have no effect on your behavior
        whatsoever

13. Which of the following is one of the Gestalt principles of
    organization?

    a. roundness
    b. isolation
    c. symmetry
    d. figure and ground

14. Monocular and binocular are two categories of

    a. distance cues
    b. size adaptations
    c. perceptual constancies
    d. visual corrections

15. When an observer moves, near objects seem to move by fast,
    intermediate objects seem to move rather slowly, and far
    objects seem to move almost not at all. The monocular cue
    explaining this is called

    a. linear perspective
    b. accommodation
    c. relative size
    d. motion parallax

16. The theory of color vision stating that there are three different color systems (red, green, and blue) is the

    a. trichromatic theory
    b. opponent-process theory
    c. tri-receptor theory
    d. lock-and-key theory

17. Which of the following is not correct?

    a. brighter objects are usually seen as closer
    b. larger objects are usually seen as farther away
    c. the object that obscures another object is seen as closer
    d. distant objects appear fuzzy because of dust and haze in the air

18. The muscular cue to distance caused by both eyes turning in or out to focus on an object is called

    a. binocular rivalry
    b. retinal disparity
    c. convergence
    d. accommodation

19. According to the Gestalt principle of proximity,

    a. objects that continue a pattern will be grouped together
    b. objects that are close together will be grouped together
    c. objects that are similar in size or shape will be grouped together
    d. there is no Gestalt principle of proximity

20. Concerning ESP (extrasensory perception), most psychologists are

    a. believers
    b. doing research supporting ESP
    c. very skeptical of ESP claims
    d. examples of people who have ESP

58

ANSWERS

<u>FILL-IN</u> <u>EXERCISES</u>

1. sensation 2. absolute threshold 3. cornea, pupil, lens, retina 4. Sound waves 5. lock-and-key 6. selection, organization, interpretation 7. size constancy
8. retinal disparity, convergence 9. trichromatic
10. precognition

<u>SAMPLE</u> <u>TEST</u> <u>QUESTIONS</u>

1.	c	11.	b
2.	c	12.	d
3.	b	13.	d
4.	a	14.	a
5.	d	15.	d
6.	a	16.	a
7.	b	17.	b
8.	d	18.	c
9.	d	19.	b
10.	d	20.	c

CHAPTER 4: CONSCIOUSNESS

OUTLINE (<u>S</u>urvey & <u>Q</u>uestion)

Use this outline when you survey the chapter, and enter your questions and comments in the space provided.

TOPIC   **NOTES**

I. STUDYING CONSCIOUSNESS

   A. Stream of Consciousness:
       The Continuously Changing
       Nature of Consciousness

   B. Levels of Awareness:
       A Continuum of
       Alertness

   C. States of Consciousness:
       Normal Versus Alternate
       States

   D. <u>Gender</u> <u>and</u> <u>Cultural</u>
       <u>Diversity</u>: Consciousness
       Across Cultures

II. SLEEP AND DREAMING

60

A. Sleep as a Biological Rhythm:
Chronobiology and the
Four Biological Rhythms

B. How Scientists Study Sleep:
Using the EEG and Sleep
Labs

C. Why Do We Sleep? Repair
or Evolutionary Advantage?

D. The Biology of Sleep:
What Causes This ASC?

E. Why Do We Dream?
Two Theories

F. Sleep Disorders:
When Sleep Becomes a
Problem

III. DRUGS AND CONSCIOUSNESS

A.   Understanding Drugs:
     How Drugs Affect
     Consciousness

B.   <u>Gender</u> <u>and</u> <u>Cultural</u>
     <u>Diversity</u>: A Cultural
     Look at Marijuana and
     Cocaine

C.   Depressants: Drugs That
     Suppress the Central
     Nervous System

D.   Stimulants: Drugs
     That Activate the
     Central Nervous System

E.   Narcotics: Drugs
     That Relieve Pain

F.   Hallucinogens: Drugs
     That Alter Perception

G.   <u>Critical</u> <u>Thinking</u>:
     Understanding Claims About
     Drug Use and Abuse

IV.   ADDITIONAL ROUTES TO
      ALTERNATE STATES

      A.   Daydreaming: A
           Special Type of
           Alternate State

      B.   Hypnosis: Alternate
           Consciousness or
           Role Playing?

      C.   Meditation:
           A "Higher" State
           of Consciousness?

LEARNING OBJECTIVES   (<u>R</u>ecite & w<u>R</u>ite)

Upon completion of Chapter 4, you should be able to:

1.   Define <u>consciousness</u> and explain what is meant by the stream
     of consciousness and levels of awareness. Compare and
     contrast normal waking consciousness and alternate states of
     consciousness (ASC).

2.   Discuss why ASCs have been of strong interest throughout
     history and across cultures. List and discuss the three
     major functions that are served by ASCs for all cultures.

3. Define <u>chronobiology</u> and describe the four biological rhythms that govern human behavior. Discuss the ill effects of disruptions in circadian rhythms.

4. Explain why electroencephalographs are used to study sleep and describe what happens in a typical night's sleep, including REM, NREM, and Stages 1, 2, 3, and 4.

5. Explain how the repair/restoration theory of sleep differs from the evolutionary/circadian theory.

6. Discuss the possible biological causes of sleep.

7. Explain the wish-fulfillment theory of dreaming and the activation-synthesis hypothesis.

8. Discuss the five major sleep disorders: insomnia, sleep apnea, narcolepsy, nightmares, and night terrors.

9. Briefly explain how drugs act as agonists or antagonists to neurotransmitters and describe the four steps of drug action on neural transmission.

10. Compare and contrast the following terms: abuse versus addiction, psychological dependence and physical dependence, withdrawal and tolerance, set and setting.

64

11. Explain how set and setting, and form and route of drug administration create differing responses in people from various cultures.

12. Define <u>depressant</u> and describe the effects of alcohol on the nervous system and behavior. Discuss why alcohol is a growing social concern.

13. Define <u>stimulant</u> and describe the effects of cocaine on the nervous system and behavior. Discuss the special problems of cocaine use.

14. Define <u>narcotic</u> and describe its effect on the nervous system and behavior. Explain why withdrawal is such a painful experience.

15. Define <u>hallucinogen</u> and describe the effects of LSD and marijuana on the nervous system and behavior.

16. Define <u>daydreaming</u> and explain why it occurs. Discuss the role of daydreams or fantasies in sexual functioning.

17. Define <u>hypnosis</u> and discuss the evidence for and against it as a separate state of consciousness.

18. Discuss the four most popular myths about hypnosis and how hypnosis has been used in medical and psychotherapy settings.

19. Define <u>meditation</u> and discuss its potential benefits.

KEY TERMS   (<u>R</u>ecite and w<u>R</u>ite)

Upon completion of Chapter 4, you should be able to define the following terms.

Activation-Synthesis Hypothesis: _____

_____

Agonist: _____

_____

Alpha Waves: _____

_____

Alternate States of Consciousness (ASCs): _____

_____

Antagonist: _____

_____

Aphrodisiacs: _____

_____

Beta Waves: _____

_____

66

Chronobiology: _____

_____

Circadian Rhythm: _____

_____

Consciousness: _____

_____

Daydreaming: _____

_____

Delta Waves: _____

_____

Depressants: _____

_____

Designer Drugs: _____

_____

Dissociation: _____

_____

Electroencephalograph (EEG): _____

_____

Evolutionary/Circadian Theory: _____

_____

Hallucinogens: _____

_____

Hypnogogic State: _____

_____

Hypnosis: _____

_____

Insomnia: _____

_____

Latent Content: _____

_____

Lucid Dreaming: _____

_____

Manifest Content: _____

_____

Meditation: _____

_____

Narcolepsy: _____

_____

Narcotics: _____

_____

Nightmares: _____

_____

Night Terrors: _____

_____

Non-Rapid Eye Movement (NREM) Sleep: _____

_____

68

Physical Dependence: _____

_____

Psychoactive Drugs: _____

_____

Psychological Dependence: _____

_____

Rapid Eye Movement (REM) Sleep: _____

_____

Repair/Restoration Theory: _____

_____

Set: _____

_____

Setting: _____

_____

Sleep Apnea: _____

_____

Stimulants: _____

_____

Synergistic Effect: _____

_____

Theta Waves: _____

_____

Tolerance: _____

_____

Wish-Fulfillment Theory: _____

_____

Withdrawal: _____

_____

FILL-IN EXERCISES   (Review & wRite)

Fill in the word or words that best fit in the spaces below.

1. Awareness of external and internal stimuli is the definition
    of _____.

2. Distortions of perceptual processes, distortions of
    emotional intensity, disruptions in normal thinking, the
    inability to communicate the experience, and feelings of
    unity and fusion are all characteristics of _____.

3. According to the _____ theory, sleep serves an important
    restorative function.

4. Sleepers deprived of _____ often exhibit a rebound effect.

5. The major sleep disorders include _____, in which a person
    has difficulty falling asleep, _____, in which a person
    has difficulty sleeping and breathing at the same time, and
    _____, in which the person has sleep attacks or excessive
    daytime sleepiness.

6. Some cultures report that _____ energizes them and
    makes them better workers. However, North Americans and
    Western Europeans often experience a mellow relaxation with
    this drug.

7. Chemicals that affect the nervous system and cause a change
    in behavior, mental processes, and conscious experience are
    referred to as _____ drugs.

8. The strongest stimulants most commonly abused are _____
    and _____.

9. _____ is an alternate state of heightened suggestibility characterized by relaxation and intense focus.

10. A group of techniques designed to focus attention and produce a heightened state of awareness is known as _____.

APPLICATION   (Recite)

Situation

When some people wake up in the morning, they feel that almost uncontrollable craving for a cup of coffee. Similarly, during the day, these individuals feel this need to always have a cup of coffee with them.

Questions to Answer

1. Why do some people express this craving for coffee?

2. What happens when they don't have that cup of coffee?

3. Do these individuals sometimes exhibit a similar craving for another product, like cigarettes or a cola drink?

4. Is this craving for coffee, cigarettes, or cola similar to the behavior exhibited by people on other drugs you read about in Chapter 4?

CRITICAL THINKING EXERCISE   (Recite)

Tolerating Ambiguity: Exploring the Meaning of Your Dreams
    (A Cognitive Skill)

Your text briefly discussed two major scientific theories and their respective attempts to explain the meaning of dreams. Unlike the popular media, which generally suggests that dreams are highly significant and easily interpreted, scientists are deeply divided about the function of dreams and their relative importance. This difference in scientific opinion provides an excellent opportunity for you to practice the critical thinking skill of <u>tolerance</u> <u>for</u> <u>ambiguity</u>. A noncritical thinker often looks for the one "right" answer or one "right" theory, whereas the critical thinker recognizes the value in competing theories and accepts that each theory may be partially correct.

To improve this critical thinking skill, begin by briefly describing your most recent and vivid dream:

_____

_____

_____

_____

Now analyze your dream using the following perspectives:

    1. According to <u>wish-fulfillment</u> <u>theory</u>, what might be the forbidden, unconscious drives or desires represented by your dream? Can you identify the manifest content versus the latent content of your dream?

    2. How would the <u>activation-synthesis</u> <u>hypothesis</u> explain your dream? Can you identify a specific thought that might have been stimulated which then led to the production of this particular dream?

    3. Psychologists such as Calvin Hall, Carl Jung, and Rosaline Cartwright suggest that analyzing your dreams can provide important personal insights, recognition of ignored or suppressed aspects of your personality, and possible solutions to real-life problems. Do you agree or disagree? Does your dream provide personal insight that increases your self-understanding?

Now that you have analyzed your dream from each perspective, can you see how difficult it is to find the one right answer? Higher level, critical thinkers recognize that competing theories are akin to the story of the four blind men who are each exploring separate parts of an elephant. By listening to their descriptions of the trunk, tail, leg, etc., critical thinkers can synthesize the information and develop a greater understanding of the larger picture.

72

SAMPLE TEST QUESTIONS   (Review)

1. The state of being aware of external and internal stimuli is referred to as

    a. an alternate state of consciousness
    b. consciousness
    c. extrasensory perception
    d. an altered state of consciousness

2. Alternate states of consciousness can be induced by

    a. drugs, sensory deprivation, sleep deprivation
    b. religious rituals, meditation, hypnosis
    c. sleep, dreaming, daydreaming
    d. all of the above

3. Which of the following is not a major function served by alternate states of consciousness?

    a. serves as a part of sacred rituals
    b. is used for social and political functions
    c. is used for individual rewards
    d. is used to treat epilepsy

4. A study of biological rhythms is called

    a. chronobiology
    b. circadian theory
    c. synchronicity
    d. biorhythmicity

5. This brain wave is associated with normal wakefulness.

    a. beta
    b. alpha
    c. theta
    d. delta

6. Which of the following statements is true?

    a. people spend about 40 percent of their sleep time
        dreaming, and about 60 percent of their waking hours
        daydreaming
    b. people spend more time daydreaming than dreaming
    c. people spend about a third of their waking time
        daydreaming and about the same percentage of sleep time
        dreaming
    d. people spend more time dreaming than daydreaming

7. Which of the following statements is supported by sleep
    research?

    a. sleep has been found to occur in three distinct stages
    b. there seem to be two distinct kinds of sleep, REM and
        NREM
    c. REM sleep occurs during the early stages of sleep
        (Stages 1 and 2)
    d. NREM sleep is absent in newborn babies

8. Which sleep theory states that sleep evolved as a means for
    conserving energy and for protecting individuals from
    predators?

    a. evolutionary/circadian theory
    b. repair/restoration theory
    c. hypnogogic theory
    d. passive theory

9. You have difficulty in going to sleep or staying asleep.
    This is known as

    a. somnambulism
    b. narcolepsy
    c. insomnia
    d. sleep apnea

10. Sudden infant death syndrome (SIDS or "crib death") may
    be caused by

    a. narcolepsy
    b. poor maternal nutrition
    c. sleep apnea
    d. parental narcolepsy

74

11. Drugs that alter conscious awareness or perception are

    a. effective in relieving psychosomatic disorders
    b. psychoactive drugs
    c. psychopharmaceutical
    d. prescribed by doctors to control hyperactivity

12. A mental desire or craving to achieve the effects produced
    by a drug is known as

    a. withdrawal effects
    b. dependency
    c. psychological dependence
    d. physical dependence

13. _____ refers to the individual's beliefs or expectations
    about drugs, while the physical and interpersonal
    environment surrounding the drug use is referred to as the
    _____.

    a. self-fulfilling prophecy, environmental setting
    b. set, setting
    c. cognitive environment, social environment
    d. set, stage

14. According to the American Medical Association, the drug that
    is the most dangerous and physically damaging is

    a. cocaine
    b. nicotine
    c. alcohol
    d. heroin

15. Drugs that block the action of specific neurotransmitters
    are called

    a. agonists
    b. antagonists
    c. hallucinogens
    d. stimulants

16. Marijuana is classified as a

    a. narcotic
    b. hallucinogen
    c. barbiturate
    d. LSD derivative

17. Which of the following drugs is a central nervous system stimulant?

    a. amphetamine
    b. alcohol
    c. heroin
    d. barbiturates

18. When street chemists take a known drug and slightly alter its molecular structure, they create what is known as

    a. a synergistic drug
    b. a street drug
    c. a designer drug
    d. crack or crank

19. A hypnotized subject who writes something but is unaware of it demonstrates the phenomenon known as

    a. age regression
    b. dissociation
    c. disinhibition
    d. mesmerism

20. Research on the effects of meditation have found

    a. increased blood pressure
    b. reductions in stress
    c. dramatic changes in perspiration
    d. an increased appetite

76

ANSWERS

FILL-IN EXERCISES

1. consciousness   2. alternate states of consciousness
3. repair/restoration   4. REM   5. insomnia,
sleep apnea, narcolepsy   6. marijuana   7. psychoactive
8. amphetamines, cocaine   9. hypnosis   10. meditation

SAMPLE TEST QUESTIONS

1.	b	11.	b
2.	d	12.	c
3.	d	13.	b
4.	a	14.	c
5.	a	15.	b
6.	c	16.	b
7.	b	17.	a
8.	a	18.	c
9.	c	19.	b
10.	c	20.	b

CHAPTER 5: LEARNING

OUTLINE (Survey & Question)

Use this outline when you survey the chapter, and enter your questions and comments in the space provided.

TOPIC	NOTES

I. LEARNED AND INNATE BEHAVIORS

    A. Learned Behavior: A Result of Experience

    B. How Do We Learn Things? Let Us Count the Ways

II. CONDITIONING

    A. Classical Conditioning: Learning Through Stimulus Pairing

    B. Operant Conditioning: Learning From Consequences

78

C. Conditioning in Action:
Using Learning Principles
in Everyday Life

D. Critical Thinking:
Operant Conditioning in
the Real World

III. COGNITIVE LEARNING

A. The Study of Insight:
Kohler's Work with
Chimpanzees

B. Latent Learning:
Tolman's "Hidden Learning"

IV. OBSERVATIONAL LEARNING

A. Gender and Cultural
Diversity: Scaffolding
as a Teaching Technique in
Different Cultures

LEARNING OBJECTIVES   (Recite & wRite)

Upon completion of Chapter 5, you should be able to:

1. Define learning.

2. Explain the difference between learned and innate behavior.

3. Describe the two major types of conditioning: classical and operant.

4. Describe cognitive learning theory and observational learning theory.

5. Understand the difference between a neutral stimulus and a conditioned stimulus in classical conditioning.

6. Explain the relationship between the conditioned stimulus, the unconditioned stimulus, the unconditioned response, and the conditioned response in classical conditioning.

7. Describe a conditioned emotional response.

8. Explain higher order conditioning.

9. Define <u>extinction</u> and <u>spontaneous recovery</u>.

10. Explain generalization and discrimination for both classical conditioning and operant conditioning.

11. Explain the differences and similarities between positive and negative reinforcement.

12. Explain the differences and similarities between positive and negative punishment.

13. Explain how negative reinforcement is not punishment.

14. Explain the difference between partial and continuous reinforcement.

15. List the different schedules of reinforcement and describe the effect these schedules will have on response rate and extinction.

16. Understand how reinforcement that is not contingent on a particular behavior can lead to superstitious behavior.

17. Explain the importance of feedback, timing, consistency, and order of presentation in the effective use of both reinforcement and punishment.

18. Define <u>shaping</u> and give an example of its use in operant conditioning.

19. Describe the conditioning principles used with biofeedback therapy and in programmed instruction.

20. Explain how insight and latent learning are examples of cognitive learning.

21. Explain the difference between observational learning and conditioning.

22. Discuss scaffolding as a teaching technique in different cultures.

KEY TERMS   (<u>R</u>ecite and w<u>R</u>ite)

Upon completion of Chapter 5, you should be able to define the following terms.

Biofeedback: _____

_____

82

Classical Conditioning: _____

_____

Cognitive Learning Theory: _____

_____

Cognitive Map: _____

_____

Conditioned Emotional Response (CER): _____

_____

Conditioned Response (CR): _____

_____

Conditioned Stimulus (CS): _____

_____

Conditioning: _____

_____

Continuous Reinforcement: _____

_____

Discrimination: _____

_____

Extinction: _____

_____

Feedback: _____

_____

Fixed Interval: _____

_____

Fixed Ratio: _____

_____

Forgetting: _____

_____

Generalization: _____

_____

Higher Order Conditioning: _____

_____

Innate: _____

_____

Insight: _____

_____

Latent Learning: _____

_____

Learned Helplessness: _____

_____

Learning: _____

_____

Modeling: _____

_____

84

Negative Punishment: _____

_____

Negative Reinforcement: _____

_____

Neutral Stimulus: _____

_____

Observational Learning Theory: _____

_____

Operant Conditioning: _____

_____

Partial Reinforcement: _____

_____

Passive Aggressiveness: _____

_____

Phobia: _____

_____

Positive Punishment: _____

_____

Positive Reinforcement: _____

_____

Primary Reinforcers: _____

_____

Programmed Instruction: _____

_____

Punishment: _____

_____

Reinforcement: _____

_____

Scaffolding: _____

_____

Schedule of Reinforcement: _____

_____

Secondary Reinforcers: _____

_____

Shaping: _____

_____

Social Learning Theory: _____

_____

Spontaneous Recovery: _____

_____

Superstitious Behavior: _____

_____

Unconditioned Response (UCR): _____

_____

Unconditioned Stimulus (UCS): _____

_____

86

Variable Interval: _____

_____

Variable Ratio: _____

_____

Vicarious Conditioning: _____

_____

FILL-IN EXERCISES   (Review & wRite)

Fill in the word or words that best fit in the spaces below.

1. A behavior that is inborn, emerges at a predetermined point of maturation, and is often triggered by some type of environmental stimulus is _____.

2. In classical conditioning, a(n) _____ is paired with a(n) _____.

3. In classical conditioning, extinction occurs when only the _____ is withheld.

4. Spontaneous recovery occurs when a previously extinguished response _____.

5. Anything that increases the probability that a particular response will be repeated is a _____.

6. Food and water are _____ reinforcers, whereas money is a _____ reinforcer.

7. The behavior of a person or animal passively enduring punishment while making no attempt to escape is called _____.

8. The best way to generate a slow, steady response rate is to use a _____ reinforcement schedule.

9. Reinforcing successive approximations to the desired behavior is called _____.

10. In most case, _____, a teaching technique in different cultures, is a combination of shaping and modeling where the teacher reinforces successes of the student and models more difficult parts of the task.

APPLICATION   (Recite)

Situation

Someone just gave you a small puppy as a gift. Needless to say, one of your responsibilities is to train the puppy to signal you when it has to go outside. To learn what to do, you read Chapter 5 in your textbook where you hope to find the necessary information to enable you to accomplish your goal.

Questions to Answer

1. Where do you start in training a puppy to signal you when it has to go outside?

2. What are some possible reinforcers you might use in training your puppy?

3. Assuming you are able to train the puppy, what schedule of reinforcement would be the least likely to produce extinction?

4. Do you think you might be able to train your puppy by having it watch another puppy that has already been trained? If so, how might this happen?

88

CRITICAL THINKING EXERCISE (<u>R</u>ecite)

<u>Applying</u> <u>Knowledge</u> <u>to</u> <u>New</u> <u>Situations</u> (A Cognitive Skill)

In Chapter 5, you learned about classical conditioning and that such learning can be applied to various situations in your own life. A critical thinker will be able to decipher the situations that are present during a learning experience. Such a thinker will also notice how often one stimulus situation is paired with another and that the two become associated with each other. However, identifying the neutral stimulus, the unconditioned stimulus (UCS), the unconditioned response (UCR), the conditioned stimulus (CS), and the conditioned response (CR) can be difficult unless you have had some practice. The following paragraphs describe classical conditioning situations. Your task is to identify the neutral stimulus, the UCS, the UCR, the CS, and the CR.

1. A researcher sounds a tone, then places a piece of meat into a dog's mouth, causing it to salivate. Eventually the sound of the tone alone causes the dog to salivate.

Neutral stimulus: _____

UCS: _____

UCR: _____

CS: _____

CR: _____

2. You have a cat that always comes running when she hears the electric can opener.

Neutral stimulus: _____

UCS: _____

UCR: _____

CS: _____

CR: _____

3. While listening to a song on his car radio, a man accidentally bumped into a red car in front of him. Thereafter, whenever he saw red cars, he experienced a severe anxiety attack.

Neutral stimulus: _____

UCS: _____

UCR: _____

CS: _____

CR: _____

SAMPLE TEST QUESTIONS (Review)

1. A relatively permanent change in behavior or behavior potential as a result of practice or experience is the definition of

   a. learning
   b. conditioning
   c. behavior modification
   d. modeling

2. Behavior that is affected by maturation only and not by practice is

   a. classically conditioned
   b. operantly conditioned
   c. innate
   d. learned via modeling

3. When your mouth waters at the sight of a chocolate cake, it is an example of

   a. operant conditioning
   b. social learning
   c. vicarious conditioning
   d. classical conditioning

4. Suppose a child learns to fear a bee by being stung when he/she touches the bee. In this situation the unconditioned stimulus is the

   a. bee
   b. sting
   c. fear
   d. crying

5. Which of the following is the proper sequence of events in classical conditioning?

   a. UCS-CS-UCR
   b. CS-UCS-UCR
   c. UCR-UCS-CS
   d. HSU-KSU-CSU

6. Higher order conditioning occurs when

   a. a previously neutral stimulus elicits a conditioned response
   b. a neutral stimulus is paired with a conditioned stimulus
   c. a neutral stimulus is paired with an unconditioned stimulus
   d. an unconditioned response is paired with a conditioned stimulus

7. In classical conditioning, extinction occurs when

   a. the conditioned stimulus is no longer paired with the unconditioned response
   b. the conditioned stimulus is no longer paired with the unconditioned stimulus
   c. the conditioned response is no longer paired with the unconditioned stimulus
   d. the unconditioned stimulus is ambiguous

8. In classical conditioning, generalization occurs when

   a. stimuli similar to the conditioned stimulus elicit the conditioned response
   b. changes in the unconditioned stimulus cause no changes in the conditioned stimulus
   c. the unconditioned stimulus elicits the unconditioned response
   d. the conditioned stimulus is paired with a neutral stimulus

9. Anything that causes an increase in a response is a(n)

    a. conditioned stimulus
    b. reinforcement
    c. punishment
    d. unconditioned stimulus

10. Anything that causes a decrease in a response is a(n)

    a. conditioned stimulus
    b. reinforcement
    c. punishment
    d. unconditioned stimulus

11. In order for reinforcement or punishment to be effective, it must come

    a. before the behavior
    b. after the behavior
    c. after the unconditioned stimulus
    d. before the unconditioned stimulus

12. Negative reinforcement and punishment are

    a. the same
    b. the best ways to learn a new behavior
    c. not the same--negative reinforcement increases behavior and punishment decreases behavior
    d. not the same, but they both decrease behavior

13. In order for extinction to occur in operant conditioning,

    a. the reinforcement must be withheld
    b. punishment must be used
    c. the conditioned stimulus must be paired with the unconditioned stimulus
    d. a secondary reinforcer must be present

14. Spontaneous recovery occurs when a

    a. previously generalized response discriminates
    b. previously extinguished response reappears
    c. behavior increases in frequency
    d. behavior has been learned and not conditioned

92

15. If you reinforce your dog for sitting by giving it a cookie every third time it sits, you are using

   a. continuous reinforcement
   b. a random ratio reinforcement schedule
   c. a fixed interval reinforcement schedule
   d. a fixed ratio reinforcement schedule

16. Superstitious behavior occurs because

   a. it has been reinforced on a fixed ratio schedule
   b. a person or an animal thinks the behavior causes a reinforcer when in reality the behavior and the reinforcement are not connected
   c. it is reinforced on a random ratio schedule
   d. the behavior and the reinforcement come in close proximity to one another, causing the superstitious behavior to increase in magnitude

17. The process of rewarding successive approximations to the desired behavior is called

   a. extinction
   b. discrimination
   c. shaping
   d. generalization

18. Which of the following is an example of cognitive learning?

   a. latent learning
   b. learning to ride a bicycle
   c. learning to eat with a fork
   d. learning to tie your shoes

19. Albert Bandura's social learning theory places a lot of emphasis on

   a. classical conditioning
   b. operant conditioning
   c. extinction
   d. modeling

20. Vicarious conditioning occurs when

   a. an animal learns from experience
   b. latent learning is exhibited
   c. a person or an animal becomes conditioned by watching a model being conditioned
   d. a person or an animal learns and then relearns the same behavior after extinction

ANSWERS

FILL-IN EXERCISES

1. innate   2. neutral stimulus, unconditioned stimulus
3. unconditioned stimulus   4. returns (reappears)
5. reinforcer or reinforcement   6. primary, secondary
7. learned helplessness   8. variable interval   9. shaping
10. scaffolding

CRITICAL THINKING EXERCISE

1. Neutral stimulus: tone
   UCS: piece of meat
   UCR: salivating
   CS: tone
   CR: salivating

2. Neutral stimulus: sound of can opener
   UCS: cat food
   UCR: running
   CS: sound of can opener
   CR: running

3. Neutral stimulus: red car
   UCS: song
   UCR: enjoyment
   CS: red car
   CR: anxiety

SAMPLE TEST QUESTIONS

1.	a	11.	b
2.	c	12.	c
3.	d	13.	a
4.	b	14.	b
5.	b	15.	d
6.	b	16.	b
7.	b	17.	c
8.	a	18.	a
9.	b	19.	d
10.	c	20.	c

CHAPTER 6: MEMORY

OUTLINE   (<u>S</u>urvey & <u>Q</u>uestion)

Use this outline when you survey the chapter, and enter your questions and comments in the space provided.

TOPIC	NOTES
I. A THREE-STAGE MEMORY MODEL	
A. Sensory Memory: The First Stage of the Process	
B. Short-Term Memory: Selecting and Concentrating	
C. Long-Term Memory: The Memory Storage System	
D. <u>Critical</u> <u>Thinking</u>: Exploring Your Memories	
E. <u>Gender</u> <u>and</u> <u>Cultural</u> <u>Diversity</u>: Cultural Differences in Memory	

96

II. THE PROBLEM OF FORGETTING

   A. Research on Forgetting:
       Factors That Affect
       Remembering

   B. Theories of Forgetting: Why
       We Don't Remember Everything

III. THE BIOLOGY OF MEMORY

   A. Theories of Memory:
       Changes in the Brain

   B. Amnesia: Trauma and
       Shock Effects

   C. Memory Impairment:
       Brain Damage

   D. Alzheimer's Disease:
       Progressive Memory Loss

IV.   EXCEPTIONAL MEMORIES

    A.   Improving Memory:
         Using Mnemonics

LEARNING OBJECTIVES   (Recite & wRite)

Upon completion of Chapter 6, you should be able to:

1.   Describe the three-stage memory model.

2.   Describe the duration and capacity of sensory memory and
     cite the importance of this stage.

3.   Describe the duration and capacity of short-term memory and
     comment on the effects of interference at this stage.

4.   Describe the way information is converted into long-term
     memory.

5.   Describe the organization, duration, and capacity of long-
     term memory.

6. Differentiate between semantic and episodic memory and give
    an example of each.

7. Differentiate among recognition, recall, and relearning
    processes. Give examples of each of these retrieval
    processes and factors influencing these including: the
    Zeigarnik effect, flashbulb memory, and eyewitness
    testimony.

8. Briefly discuss the effects of serial position, massed
    practice, and distributed practice on memory.

9. Define <u>state-dependent</u> <u>memory</u> and give an example.

10. Differentiate between proactive and retroactive interference
    in memory processing.

11. Compare the decay and interference theories of forgetting.

12. Give an example of motivated forgetting and contrast this
    process to amnesias from brain trauma.

13. Discuss the retrieval failure theory of forgetting.

14. Describe the effects of brain trauma and ECS.

15. Differentiate between retrograde and anterograde amnesia.

16. Briefly describe the brain changes in Alzheimer's disease and relate these to the behavioral changes.

17. Describe eidetic imagery and relate it to the stages of the memory model.

18. Give examples of mnemonic devices and relate these strategies to the dual-code theory of memory.

KEY TERMS   (Recite and wRite)

Upon completion of Chapter 6, you should be able to define the following terms.

Alzheimer's Disease: _____

_____

100

Amnesia: _____

_____

Anterograde Amnesia: _____

_____

Chunking: _____

_____

Cue: _____

_____

Decay Theory: _____

_____

Distributed Practice: _____

_____

Dual-Coding System: _____

_____

Eidetic Imagery: _____

_____

Electroconvulsive Shock (ECS): _____

_____

Episodic Memory: _____

_____

Flashbulb Memories: _____

_____

Interference Task: _____

_____

Interference Theory: _____

_____

Landmark Events: _____

_____

Levels of Processing: _____

_____

Long-Term Memory (LTM): _____

_____

Long-Term Potentiation (LTP): _____

_____

Maintenance Rehearsal: _____

_____

Massed Practice: _____

_____

Method of Loci: _____

_____

Method of Word Associations: _____

_____

Mnemonic Devices: _____

_____

Motivated Forgetting Theory: _____

_____

Peg-Word Mnemonic System: _____

_____

102

Proactive Interference: _____

_____

Recall: _____

_____

Recognition: _____

_____

Redintegration: _____

_____

Relearning: _____

_____

Retrieval: _____

_____

Retrieval Failure Theory: _____

_____

Retroactive Interference: _____

_____

Retrograde Amnesia: _____

_____

Reverberating Circuits: _____

_____

Selective Attention: _____

_____

Semantic Memory: _____

_____

Sensory Memory: _____

_____

Serial Position Effect: _____

_____

Short-Term Memory (STM): _____

_____

State-Dependent Memory: _____

_____

Substitute Word System: _____

_____

Tip-of-the-Tongue (TOT): _____

_____

Zeigarnik Effect: _____

_____

FILL-IN EXERCISES   (Review & wRite)

Fill in the word or words that best fit in the spaces below.

1. The three types of memory that are part of the memory model
    are _____, _____, and _____.

2. The process of _____ enables us to store more information
    in short-term memory (STM) by grouping things into separate
    units.

3. Processing of information both visually and verbally is
    called a _____ system.

4. Knowledge of facts and how they relate to one another are
    stored in a special long-term memory (LTM) called _____
    memory.

5. A second type of LTM that contains autobiographical information is called _____ memory.

6. We know that people in _____ cultures are forced to rely soley on their memories to recall past information-- information about history and commerce, for instance.

7. The _____ is the effect experienced when we remember things at the ends of a list but forget things in the middle of the list.

8. Memories that are associated with a particular level of emotional arousal are called _____ memories.

9. In retrograde amnesia, a person has difficulty remembering events that occurred _____ the brain disruption.

10. The scientific name of photographic memory is _____ .

APPLICATION   (<u>R</u>ecite)

<u>Situation</u>

Instead of keeping up with the reading for the course, you have delayed most of it until the night before the exam. You are now faced with having to read four chapters and you have very little time to do it. As you begin to read the chapters, it all starts to look the same and confusion begins to set in. Further, you realize that as you progress through your reading you remember very little of what you just read. You realize that you have created an almost impossible situation for yourself and you fear you will fail the exam.

<u>Questions</u> <u>to</u> <u>Answer</u>

1. Why is all the material starting to look the same?

2. What could you have done to prevent this?

3. Are there any methods you might still use to get you through the exam?

4. What advice would you give fellow classmates concerning your present experience?

CRITICAL THINKING EXERCISE (R̲ecite)

Employing̲ Precise̲ Terms̲ (A Cognitive Skill)

In Chapter 6, you learned about different reasons why forgetting occurs. A critical thinker should be able to identify a specific theory that applies to a given situation. Below you will find the names of forgetting theories. Identify which of these theories seems most likely to apply to the examples of forgetting that follow.

Theories̲ of̲ Forgetting̲

Interference theory
Decay theory
Motivated forgetting theory
Retrieval failure theory

   1. A close friend of yours told you that she has no memory of her father. When discussing this with her mother, you discover that the father no longer lives with them because he molested your friend when she was a child.

_____

   2. You can't remember something during an examination, but recall it after you turn in the test and leave the room.

_____

   3. When you try to recall the French vocabulary you studied last night, you remember some Spanish vocabulary words you learned several years ago.

_____

   4. When you were in the 8th grade talent show, you made a fool of yourself in front of the entire student body. You were so embarrassed that you had completely forgotten about it until an old friend reminds you when you two are reminiscing about "old times."

_____

106

5. You can't remember the last name of a good friend when introducing her to another friend. After they leave, the name pops into your mind.

_____

SAMPLE TEST QUESTIONS   (Review)

1. A visual image in sensory memory

    a. lasts about 1/2 second
    b. lasts longer than sounds remain in this stage
    c. contains only the images that have been selected for our attention
    d. is always processed into STM

2. STM is also referred to as

    a. sensory memory
    b. eidetic imagery
    c. photographic memory
    d. working memory

3. Maintenance rehearsal

    a. causes consolidation
    b. prevents chunking
    c. reenters information in sensory memory
    d. reenters information in STM

4. Information is stored in LTM when _____ takes place.

    a. maintenance rehearsal
    b. chunking
    c. consolidation
    d. organization

5. Chunking enables a person to

    a. select contents from sensory memory
    b. organize contents of STM
    c. organize contents of LTM
    d. use dual coding in sensory memory

6. The two-part division of STM is referred to as a

    a. sensory-coding system
    b. perceptual-coding system
    c. retrieval-coding system
    d. dual-coding system

7. Facts are stored in

    a. sensory memory
    b. STM
    c. semantic memory
    d. episodic memory

8. Landmark events enable us to locate information in

    a. semantic memory
    b. episodic memory
    c. sensory memory
    d. STM

9. Which of the following is a recognition test of memory?

    a. remembering a name that goes with a face
    b. a multiple choice test
    c. an essay test
    d. remembering the names of the capitals of states

10. Research on flashbulb memories has found that

    a. once a memory is stored in LTM, it is not changed
    b. stored memories can be modified before or after consolidation
    c. inferences or assumptions are not added to information with a strong emotional impact
    d. if a memory is vivid, it is an accurate account of the original experience

11. According to the decay theory of forgetting, we are unable to remember information

    a. if it has been replaced with newer information
    b. when it has deteriorated with the passage of time
    c. of negative emotional impact
    d. when we are in a emotional state different from that we were in when we learned that information

108

12. If during a French test in college you remember some
    Spanish words you learned in high school, these previously
    learned words would be causing _____ interference.

    a. retroactive
    b. proactive
    c. chunking
    d. semantic

13. The activity of reverberating circuits is believed to
    account for the qualities of

    a. sensory memory
    b. STM
    c. LTM
    d. photographic memory

14. The process whereby short-term memories become long-term
    memories after repeated stimulation of a synapse that leads
    to chemical and structural changes in the dendrites of the
    receiving neuron is known as

    a. long-term potentiation
    b. reverberation
    c. kinases
    d. electroconvulsion

15. John was unable to remember the events occurring just before
    his automobile accident. This memory loss from brain trauma
    is known as _____ amnesia.

    a. anterograde
    b. retrograde
    c. proactive
    d. retroactive

16. Electroconvulsive shock prevents

    a. the operation of sensory memory
    b. selection of information from sensory memory
    c. consolidation
    d. retrograde amnesia

17. The patient H. M. was unable to consolidate information from STM after surgical removal of portions of his

    a. occipital lobes
    b. subcortex
    c. frontal lobes
    d. temporal lobes

18. In Alzheimer's disease, the amount of _____ produced by brain tissue is decreased.

    a. cerebrospinal fluid
    b. hydrochloric acid
    c. dopamine
    d. acetylcholine

19. Photographic memory enables a person to store a complete visual image rather than the limited amount of information normally selected for attention in

    a. sensory memory
    b. STM
    c. LTM
    d. intermediate memory

20. The method of loci mnemonic system uses _____ to organize information to be learned.

    a. images of physical locations
    b. substitute words
    c. images of objects to represent numbers
    d. numbers

110

ANSWERS

FILL-IN EXERCISES

1. sensory memory, short-term memory (STM), long-term memory (LTM)   2. chunking   3. dual-coding   4. semantic
5. episodic   6. preliterate   7. serial position effect
8. state-dependent   9. before   10. eidetic imagery

CRITICAL THINKING EXERCISE

1. motivated forgetting theory   2. retrieval failure theory
3. interference theory   4. motivated forgetting theory
5. retrieval failure theory

SAMPLE TEST QUESTIONS

1.	a	11.	b
2.	d	12.	b
3.	d	13.	b
4.	c	14.	a
5.	b	15.	b
6.	d	16.	c
7.	c	17.	d
8.	b	18.	d
9.	b	19.	b
10.	b	20.	a

CHAPTER 7:   THINKING AND INTELLIGENCE

OUTLINE   (Survey & Question)

Use this outline when you survey the chapter, and enter your questions and comments in the space provided.

| TOPIC | NOTES |

I.   THINKING

A.   How Do We Think?
Pictures and Words

B.   Mental Imagery: Thinking
in Pictures, Sounds,
Smells . . .

C.   Concepts: How We
Organize Knowledge

D.   Problem Solving:
Moving From a Given
State to a Goal State

E. Creativity: Finding
Unique Solutions to Problems

F. Critical Thinking:
Solving Everyday Problems

G. Language and Thought: A
Complex Interaction

II. INTELLIGENCE AND INTELLIGENCE TESTING

A. Intelligence Defined:
More Difficult Than It
Seems

B. Measuring Intelligence:
What Constitutes a
Good Test?

C. IQ Tests: Predictors
of School Performance

D. <u>Gender</u> <u>and</u> <u>Cultural</u>
<u>Diversity</u>: Cultural
Differences in School
Success

E. Differences in Intelligence:
How and Why We Are Different

F. Heredity Versus Environment:
Which Determines Intelligence?

LEARNING OBJECTIVES   (<u>R</u>ecite & w<u>R</u>ite)

Upon completion of Chapter 7, you should be able to:

1. Define <u>cognition</u> and <u>thinking</u>.

2. Compare and contrast the information processing approach
with the connectionist approach to studying cognition.

3. Describe how mental images are used in information
processing.

114

4. Describe the dual-coding hypothesis and its relationship to the use of mental images.

5. Define <u>concepts</u> and explain how humans use concepts.

6. Describe the hypothesis-testing theory and the prototype theory of concept formation.

7. List the three stages of problem solving and explain what type of thinking goes on at each stage.

8. List and explain the most common barriers to problem solving.

9. Explain why creativity is associated with fluency, flexibility, and originality.

10. Describe several research projects that have involved attempts to teach language to animals.

11. Describe phonemes, morphemes, grammar, and syntax and their role in language.

12. Define <u>intelligence</u>.

13. Differentiate between fluid intelligence and crystallized intelligence.

14. Describe Sternberg's triarchic theory of human intelligence.

15. Discuss the need for standardization in the use of IQ tests.

16. Define <u>reliability</u> and <u>validity</u> and explain why they are important for IQ tests.

17. Describe the Stanford-Binet IQ test and what this test is designed to measure.

18. Describe the Wechsler intelligence tests.

19. Discuss some of the abuses of IQ tests.

20. Discuss some of the causes of mental retardation.

116

21. Discuss the issue of mainstreaming versus special placement.

22. Discuss mental giftedness and how individuals in this category are identified.

23. Discuss the issue of environment versus heredity as the source of individual differences in IQ scores.

KEY TERMS   (<u>R</u>ecite and w<u>R</u>ite)

Upon completion of Chapter 7, you should be able to define the following terms.

Algorithm: _____

_____

Attributes: _____

_____

Brainstorming: _____

_____

Cognition: _____

_____

Concept: _____

_____

Connectionist Approach: _____

_____

Convergent Thinking: _____

_____

Creativity: _____

_____

Crystallized Intelligence: _____

_____

Divergent Thinking: _____

_____

Dual-Coding Hypothesis: _____

_____

Evaluation: _____

_____

Fluid Intelligence: _____

_____

Functional Fixedness: _____

_____

Grammar: _____

_____

Heuristics: _____

_____

Incubation: _____

_____

Information Processing Approach: _____

_____

118

Intelligence: _____

_____

Intelligence Quotient (IQ): _____

_____

Language: _____

_____

Mental Images: _____

_____

Morpheme: _____

_____

Phoneme: _____

_____

Preparation: _____

_____

Problem Solving: _____

_____

Problem-Solving Set: _____

_____

Production: _____

_____

Prototype: _____

_____

Reliability: _____

_____

Standardization: _____

_____

Syntax: _____

_____

Thinking: _____

_____

Validity: _____

_____

FILL-IN EXERCISES   (<u>R</u>eview & w<u>R</u>ite)

Fill in the word or words that best fit in the spaces below.

1. The _____ approach to cognition is based on abstract
    models of human cognition rather than trying to directly
    model how the brain works.

2. There is quite a controversy over how we think, but research
    tends to support the _____, which proposes that
    information is coded via both an imagery system and a verbal
    system.

3. The three stages that a person must pass through in order to
    solve a problem are _____, _____, and _____.

4. According to J. P. Guilford, creative thinking is associated
    with _____, _____, and _____.

5. The basic speech sounds /ch/ and /v/ are known as _____;
    the smallest meaningful units of language such as "ing" and
    "book" are known as _____.

6. _____ intelligence refers to our ability to gain new
    knowledge and to attack and solve novel problems.

7. A test is _____ if a person scores the same on a retest as
    he/she did on the first test.

8. An intelligence quotient (IQ) is the ratio of a child's
    _____ age to a child's _____ age times 100.

9. One major difference between the Stanford-Binet and the
    Wechsler intelligence tests is that the Wechsler tests give
    both a _____ and a _____ score.

10. _____ is an example of organic retardation that results
    from an extra chromosome in the body's cells.

APPLICATION   (Recite)

Situation

You have been asked to develop your own intelligence test and to
include items that you think should be on such a test. However,
you know that good tests already exist to assess intelligence.
Nonetheless, you begin to read about intelligence to see if you
can develop a very short version of an intelligence test.

Questions to Answer

1. Do you think you can develop your own intelligence test?

2. What are the important criteria you must consider to have a
    good intelligence test?

3. Are there any areas of intelligence that you think need to
    be included on your test that may not be on existing tests?

4. What would you do to make your test culture-free?

CRITICAL THINKING EXERCISE   (Recite)

Metacognition   (A Cognitive Skill)

Metacognition, also known as reflective or recursive thinking,
involves a review and analysis of your own mental processes--
thinking about your own thinking. Below is a problem that
involves this type of critical thinking. Take a few minutes and
work on it.

Problem

There is a bird, Tweety, that likes to perch on the roof of Casey Jones, a locomotive that travels the 200-mile route from Cucamonga to Kalamazoo. As Casey Jones pulls out from Cucamonga, the bird takes to the air and flies to Kalamazoo, the train's destination. Because the train travels at only 50 mph whereas the bird travels at 100 mph, Tweety reaches Kalamazoo before the train and finds that it has nowhere to perch. So the bird flies back to the train and finds it still moving, whereupon Tweety flies back to Kalamazoo, then back to the train, and so on until Casey Jones finally arrives in Kalamazoo, where the bird finally rests on the locomotive's roof. How far has the bird flown?

Now that you've had your fun working the problem above, this is an exercise to apply what you've learned in your textbook about the steps you used in solving the problem. In the blanks below, first fill in the name of the step, then describe the processes you used during each step in solving the above problem. Make sure you include the following terms, if applicable:

algorithm	creating subgoals	evaluation
given facts	goal	heuristics
hypothesis	incubation	means-end analysis
preparation	production	working backward

Step 1: _____

    Procedure: _____

_____

_____

_____

Step 2: _____

    Procedure: _____

_____

_____

_____

122

Step 3: _____

Procedure: _____

_____

_____

_____

SAMPLE TEST QUESTIONS   (Review)

1. This model of cognition claims that in order for the brain to analyze and process the immense amount of information bombarding it every minute, it must do many different things at once.

    a. information processing model
    b. connectionist model
    c. concept model
    d. serial processing model

2. A mental structure used to categorize things that share similar characteristics is a

    a. problem
    b. solution
    c. concept
    d. percept

3. This theory of concept formation proposes that in real life, our concepts are organized in terms of best examples.

    a. dual-coding theory
    b. hypothesis-testing theory
    c. prototype theory
    d. attribution theory

4. Preparation, production, and evaluation are the three major steps in

   a. problem solving
   b. cognition
   c. thinking
   d. artificial intelligence

5. What are the two major methods used in generating hypotheses for solving problems?

   a. factor analysis and analysis of variance
   b. insight and meditation
   c. insight and deduction
   d. algorithms and heuristics

6. Which of the following is an algorithm?

   a. a fixed ratio reinforcement schedule
   b. dream analysis
   c. 3 X 10 is 10 + 10 + 10
   d. you can usually get the correct answer faster if you ask the smartest person in your classroom

7. Failing to solve a problem because of an inability to see novel uses for a familiar object is

   a. problem-solving set
   b. functional fixedness
   c. heuristics
   d. incubation

8. According to J. P. Guilford, which of the following are the three abilities associated with creativity?

   a. fluency, vocabulary, experience
   b. fluency, flexibility, originality
   c. flexibility, heuristics, algorithms
   d. originality, fluency, experience

124

9. _____ is the group problem solving technique in which the following rules are followed: 1) no criticism; 2) create as many solutions as possible; 3) encourage originality; 4) try to build on previous ideas.

    a. Divergent thinking
    b. Insight
    c. Connectionism
    d. Brainstorming

10. Benjamin Whorf proposed that

    a. language is not natural and must be learned
    b. the structure of language can influence people's behavior
    c. American Sign Language is not a natural language
    d. language development is genetically predetermined

11. The basic speech sounds are called

    a. morphemes
    b. phonemes
    c. syntax
    d. images

12. The capacity to solve problems and to adapt readily to a changing environment is the definition of

    a. IQ
    b. intelligence
    c. artificial intelligence
    d. creativity

13. If a test gives you the same score each time you take the test, that test would be

    a. reliable
    b. valid
    c. standardized
    d. useless

14. Validity refers to the ability of a test to

    a. return the same score on separate administrations of the test
    b. predict what it is designed to predict
    c. not to discriminate between different cultural groups
    d. give a standard deviation of scores

15. IQ tests are mainly

    a. general intelligence tests
    b. achievement tests
    c. tests of academic ability
    d. graduate school entrance examinations

16. Which of the following is an individual intelligence test?

    a. Stanford-Binet
    b. SAT
    c. ACT
    d. AFQT

17. According to Sternberg's triarchic theory of intelligence, the three aspects of intelligence are:

    a. internal components, adaptation to change through use of our internal components, and application of past experience to problem solving
    b. external components, adaptation to change through use of our external components, and application of present experience to problem solving
    c. internal components, adaptation to change through use of our external components, and application of future expectancies for problem solving
    d. external components, adaptation to change through use of our internal components, and application of present knowledge

18. Which of the following would be most likely to have similar IQ test scores?

    a. identical twins raised apart
    b. identical twins raised together
    c. fraternal twins raised apart
    d. brothers and sisters from the same parents

19. Stemming from their days as pre-Civil War slaves, African Americans have become reconciled to hearing others undermine their abilities--so much so that they fall into the delusion that they actually are incapable of succeeding in school. This is referred to as the

    a. low-effort syndrome
    b. low-esteem syndrome
    c. no-esteem syndrome
    d. failure syndrome

126

20. When developmentally delayed youngsters are integrated into regular classrooms with predominantly nonhandicapped children, they are said to be

   a. accelerated
   b. special placed
   c. mainstreamed
   d. mainlined

ANSWERS

<u>FILL-IN</u> <u>EXERCISES</u>

1. information processing   2. dual-coding hypothesis
3. preparation, production, evaluation   4. fluency,
flexibility, originality 5. phonemes, morphemes
6. Fluid   7. reliable 8. mental, chronological
9. verbal, performance   10. Down syndrome

<u>SAMPLE</u> <u>TEST</u> <u>QUESTIONS</u>

1.	b	11.	b
2.	c	12.	b
3.	c	13.	a
4.	a	14.	b
5.	d	15.	c
6.	c	16.	a
7.	b	17.	a
8.	b	18.	b
9.	d	19.	a
10.	b	20.	c

CHAPTER 8:   LIFE SPAN DEVELOPMENT

OUTLINE   (<u>S</u>urvey & <u>Q</u>uestion)

Use this outline when you survey the chapter, and enter your questions and comments in the space provided.

TOPIC	NOTES

I.   STUDYING DEVELOPMENT

    A.   <u>Gender</u> <u>and</u> <u>Cultural</u> <u>Diversity</u>:   Cultural Psychology's Guidelines for Developmental Research

II.   PHYSICAL DEVELOPMENT

    A.   Prenatal Development: From Conception to Birth

    B.   <u>Gender</u> <u>and</u> <u>Cultural</u> <u>Diversity</u>:   A Cultural Comparison of Prenatal and Infant Health Care

C.   Postnatal Development:
     Early Childhood, Adolescence,
     and Adulthood

III.   LANGUAGE DEVELOPMENT

IV.   COGNITIVE DEVELOPMENT

A.   Stages of Cognitive
     Development: Birth
     to Adolescence

B.   Assessing Piaget's Theory:
     Criticisms and Contributions

C.   Critical Thinking:
     Developing Insight
     into Egocentricity

V.   MORAL DEVELOPMENT

130

A. <u>Gender</u> and <u>Cultural</u>
<u>Diversity</u>: Insights Into
Morality From Cross-Cultural
Studies and Gilligan's Research

VI. GENDER DEVELOPMENT

VII. SOCIAL AND PERSONALITY DEVELOPMENT

A. Attachment: The Beginnings
of Love

B. Parenting Styles: The
Effects of Different
Child-Rearing Methods

C. Erikson's Psychosocial Theory:
The Eight Stages of Life

D. Myths of Development:
Stormy Adolescence, Midlife
Crisis, and Empty Nest

VIII.   SPECIAL ISSUES IN DEVELOPMENT

A.   Families: Their Effect
     on Development

B.   Occupational Choices:
     The Effect of Work and
     Careers

C.   Death and Dying:
     Another Stage in
     Development?

LEARNING OBJECTIVES   (Recite & wRite)

Upon completion of Chapter 8, you should be able to:

1.   Define developmental psychology and discuss the research
     issues of nature versus nurture, continuity versus stages,
     and stability versus change.

2.   Distinguish between cross-sectional and longitudinal
     research techniques.

132

3. Discuss the four major points made by cultural psychologists regarding the impact of culture on human development.

4. List the three stages of prenatal development and describe the major physical changes associated with each stage.

5. Discuss the effects of nutrition and drugs on prenatal development. Explain why the United States has such a high infant mortality rate.

6. Briefly describe the major changes in brain, motor, and sensory and perceptual development during the prenatal period and in the first few months of life.

7. Briefly describe the major physical changes that occur during adolescence.

8. Briefly describe the major physical changes that occur during middle age and late adulthood. Define primary aging and secondary aging and discuss the two major theories regarding what causes aging and death.

9. Discuss how children communicate nonverbally. Explain Darwin's position on the innate nature of infant emotional expression.

10. Briefly describe the characteristics of the prelinguistic and linguistic stages of language development.

11. Compare and contrast the nature versus nurture positions on language development.

12. Discuss Piaget's approach to cognitive development and define the terms <u>adaptation</u>, <u>schemata</u>, <u>assimilation</u>, and <u>accommodation</u>.

13. List and describe Piaget's four stages of cognitive development.

14. Discuss the two major criticisms of Piaget's theory and describe his contributions.

134

15. List and describe Kohlberg's three levels of moral development and give examples of typical reasoning at each stage.

16. Discuss criticisms of Kohlberg's theory of moral development.

17. Define gender, gender identity, and gender role. Briefly describe gender-schema theory.

18. Define attachment and discuss research evidence supporting its possible biological basis.

19. Briefly describe the findings of Harlow's research with rhesus monkeys on contact comfort and discuss how these findings may apply to human relationships.

20. Discuss Ainsworth's research on levels of attachment among infants and their mothers. Compare this research with Hazen and Shaver's findings regarding adult love relationships.

21. List and describe Baumrind's three parenting styles and discuss the effects on children who grow up with each parenting style. Discuss the contributions of cross-cultural research to the study of parenting styles and child development.

22. Briefly describe the eight stages of life according to Erikson's psychosocial theory. Evaluate the criticism of Erikson's theory.

23. Discuss the three major myths of development: adolescence "storm and stress", midlife crisis, and the empty nest syndrome.

24. Discuss the impact of child abuse, teenage parents, and divorce on personality and social development.

25. Describe the effects of occupational choice on development.

26. Briefly describe Kubler-Ross's five-stage theory of the process of death and dying and relate her concepts to the hospice movement.

136

KEY TERMS   (Recite and wRite)

Upon completion of Chapter 8, you should be able to define the following terms.

Accommodation: _____

_____

Adaptation: _____

_____

Adolescence: _____

_____

Adolescent Egocentrism: _____

_____

Androgens: _____

_____

Animism: _____

_____

Assimilation: _____

_____

Attachment: _____

_____

Babbling: _____

_____

Care Perspective: _____

_____

Chromosomes: _____

_____

Cohort Effects: _____

_____

Conception: _____

_____

Concrete Operational Stage: _____

_____

Conservation: _____

_____

Conventional Level: _____

_____

Cross-Sectional Method: _____

_____

Developmental Psychology: _____

_____

Egocentrism: _____

_____

Embryonic Period: _____

_____

Empty Nest Syndrome: _____

_____

Estrogens: _____

_____

138

Fetal Alcohol Syndrome: _____

_____

Fetal Period: _____

_____

Formal Operational Period: _____

_____

Gender: _____

_____

Gender Identity: _____

_____

Gender Role: _____

_____

Gender Role Stereotypes: _____

_____

Generalization: _____

_____

Genes: _____

_____

Germinal Period: _____

_____

Imprinting: _____

_____

Interactionist Model: _____

_____

Justice Perspective: _____

_____

Language Acquisition Device (LAD): _____

_____

Longitudinal Method: _____

_____

Male Climacteric: _____

_____

Maturation: _____

_____

Menopause: _____

_____

Midlife Crisis: _____

_____

Myelination: _____

_____

Object Permanence: _____

_____

Operations: _____

_____

Overextension: _____

_____

Overgeneralize: _____

_____

140

Postconventional Level: _____

_____

Preconventional Level: _____

_____

Preoperational Stage: _____

_____

Primary Aging: _____

_____

Psychosocial Stages of Development: _____

_____

Puberty: _____

_____

Reflexes: _____

_____

Schemata: _____

_____

Secondary Aging: _____

_____

Secondary Sex Characteristics: _____

_____

Sensorimotor Stage: _____

_____

Sex: _____

_____

Stereotype: _____

_____

Storm and Stress: _____

_____

Telegraphic Speech: _____

_____

Teratogen: _____

_____

Thanatology: _____

_____

FILL-IN EXERCISES   (<u>R</u>eview & w<u>R</u>ite)

Fill in the word or words that best fit in the spaces below.

1.   _____ involves the description, explanation, prediction, and modification of age-related behaviors from conception to death.

2.   The debate over whether behavior is primarily learned or inborn is known as the _____ controversy.

3.   In the United States, _____ infants are twice as likely as _____ infants to be born prematurely, to have low birth weight, and to die in the first year of life.

4.   _____ occurs when existing schemata are used to interpret new information, whereas _____ involves changes and adaptations of the schemata.

5. During the _____ stage of development, the child understands and applies logical operations to concrete, external objects.

6. According to Kohlberg, individuals at the _____ level of morality tend to judge right and wrong on the basis of the consequences (reward or punishment).

7. Gilligan's term for an approach to moral reasoning that emphasizes individual rights and views people as differentiated and standing alone is referred to as _____.

8. The term _____ refers to the social components of being male or female while _____ refers to how one psychologically perceives oneself as either male or female.

9. In the _____ level of attachment, the infant becomes very upset as the mother leaves the room.

10. Elizabeth Kubler-Ross's five stages of dying are _____, _____, _____, _____, and _____.

APPLICATION (Recite)

Situation

A brother and a sister are playing in their backyard when one of them spots something flying. He remarks, "Look at the birdie!" The sister replies, "That's not a birdie, it's an airplane!"

Questions to Answer

1. Why would one child mistake an airplane for a bird?

2. How old would you guess the child to be who mistook the airplane for a bird?

3. When are children able to distinguish between different flying objects?

4. When children can distinguish different flying objects, what else are they capable of cognitively doing at that age?

CRITICAL THINKING EXERCISE   (<u>R</u>ecite)

<u>Thinking</u> <u>Independently</u>: <u>Making</u> <u>Peace</u> <u>With</u> <u>Your</u> <u>Parents</u>
    (An Affective Skill)

One mark of a critical thinker is the ability to think
independently, which requires insight into one's own beliefs.
When we feel at peace with people, we can consider their beliefs
in an untroubled way and espouse them as our own or reject them
freely. The following exercise will help you to clarify how
psychologically independent you are from your parents by asking
you to focus on your relationship with them. Many people
consider independence to be merely financial. However,
psychological independence is an equally significant mark of adult
development. Hopefully, exploring your relationship with your
parents will help you to become independent of them, as a
critical thinker and as a person. In that regard, take a few
moments to jot down your answers to the following:

1.   Are you truly free of regrets and resentments from your
     childhood?

2.   Are you relaxed and do you enjoy spending time with your
     parents? Or do you resent "having" to visit or interact
     with them?

3.   Are you able to accept your parents, forgive them their
     mistakes, and give up trying to change them?

4.   Do you feel loved and accepted by your parents?

5.   Do you still compare yourself and compete with one of your
     brothers or sisters?

6.   Are you still waiting to escape from your parents' rules,
     influence, or habits to become your own person?

144

7. Are you glad you had the parents you did?

8. If your parents are divorced, have you resolved your mixed feelings about this situation?

9. Do you have fears of being trapped or disappointed by a committed love relationship or marriage in your own life?

10. Have you completed your resentments and regrets toward your parent who may no longer be living? Can you accept the reality and inevitability of your own death?

Your answers to each of these questions are an important first step in actually recognizing and eventually working through these long-standing problems. These questions were adapted from the paperback book <u>Making</u> <u>Peace</u> <u>With</u> <u>Your</u> <u>Parents</u> by Harold H. Bloomfield, M.D. and Leonard Felder, Ph.D. (New York: Ballantine Books, 1983). If you desire further specific self-help information on this topic, this book is a wonderful resource. For those of you who are reading this and feeling overwhelmed by the magnitude of your problems with your parents, you may want to seek professional psychological counseling, and your instructor may be able to recommend someone in your area.

SAMPLE TEST QUESTIONS   (<u>R</u>eview)

1. Developmental psychologists are <u>not</u> interested in

   a. age-related behaviors across the entire life span
   b. the relative contributions of both nature and nurture
   c. the cognitive, physical, and social changes that occur during development
   d. developing job-preference tests

2. Conception occurs when

   a. a fertilized egg implants in the uterine lining
   b. the ovum undergoes its first cell division
   c. ejaculation occurs
   d. a sperm cell unites with an ovum

3. The period of life when an individual first becomes capable of reproduction is known as

   a. the growth spurt
   b. adolescence
   c. puberty
   d. the latency period

4. Menopause is

   a. another name for the onset of the menstrual cycle
   b. a time of wild mood swings for all women due to fluctuations in hormones
   c. the cessation of the menstrual cycle
   d. the result of increases in estrogen levels

5. Male climacteric refers to

   a. the cessation of testosterone production
   b. the end of male reproductive abilities
   c. physical and psychological changes of middle age
   d. the beginning of sexual potency

6. "I goed to the zoo" and "I hurted myself" are examples of

   a. prelinguistic verbalizations
   b. overexposure to adult "baby talk"
   c. overgeneralization
   d. Noam Chomsky's theory of language acquisition

7. Which of the following statements best reflects Jean Piaget's view of cognitive development?

   a. children's cognitive abilities are quantitatively different from adults'
   b. children's cognitive abilities are qualitatively different from adults'
   c. children's cognitive understanding is primarily a reflection of the environment
   d. conditioning principles best explain a child's cognitive growth

8. Piaget used the term <u>egocentrism</u> to describe the fact that

   a. all children are naturally selfish during the first few years of life
   b. children view the world from one perspective (their own)
   c. the child's limited logic impedes his or her understanding of the need to share
   d. the child's inability to conserve

9. During Piaget's fourth stage of cognitive development, adolescents first become capable of

   a. egocentrism
   b. dealing effectively with transformations
   c. using language and other symbols
   d. hypothetical thinking

10. Bill refuses to go to the dance because he's afraid everyone will notice that he could not afford a new suit. His fears most clearly demonstrate

   a. formal operational thinking
   b. peer pressure
   c. adolescent egocentrism
   d. adolescent ethnocentrism

11. During Kohlberg's _____ level of moral development, right and wrong are judged on the basis of consequences.

   a. conventional
   b. amoral
   c. postconventional
   d. preconventional

12. Gilligan's term for an approach in moral reasoning that emphasizes individual rights and views people as differentiated and standing alone is the _____.

   a. justice perspective
   b. care perspective
   c. liability perspective
   d. amortization perspective

13. How one psychologically perceives oneself as either male or female is referred to as _____.

    a. sex role
    b. gender
    c. gender identity
    d. gender role

14. According to this theory, children use gender as a schema to organize and guide their view of the world.

    a. moral-development theory
    b. cognitive-development theory
    c. psychosocial theory
    d. gender-schema theory

15. Harlow's research with infant monkeys and artificial surrogate mothers indicates

    a. that the most important factor in infant development is a loving environment
    b. that attachment is not essential to normal development
    c. no significant difference in the choice of wire or terrycloth mothers
    d. that the most important variable in attachment may be contact comfort

16. This type of parenting style involves parents who value unquestioning obedience and mature responsibility from their children, while remaining aloof and detached.

    a. authoritarian
    b. permissive-indifferent
    c. permissive-indulgent
    d. authoritative

17. The first of Erikson's eight stages of psychosocial development is concerned with

    a. autonomy versus shame and doubt
    b. initiative versus guilt
    c. trust versus mistrust
    d. identity versus role confusion

18. This possible "myth of development" involves a painful separation and depression that parents supposedly feel when their last child leaves home.

    a. the midlife crisis
    b. the empty nest syndrome
    c. "storm and stress"
    d. linear development

19. Teenage pregnancy is usually associated with all but the following.

    a. lower educational achievement
    b. increased esteem
    c. reduced economic opportunities
    d. impaired marital opportunities

20. According to Elizabeth Kubler-Ross, which of the following is not one of the stages that people go through while coping with death?

    a. retrenchment
    b. denial
    c. anger
    d. bargaining

ANSWERS

FILL-IN EXERCISES

1. Developmental psychology   2. nature versus nurture
3. black, white   4. assimilation, accommodation
5. concrete operational   6. preconventional, conventional
7. justice perspective   8. gender, gender identity
9. anxious-ambivalent   10. denial, anger, bargaining, depression, acceptance

SAMPLE TEST QUESTIONS

1.	d	11.	d
2.	d	12.	a
3.	c	13.	c
4.	c	14.	d
5.	c	15.	d
6.	c	16.	a
7.	b	17.	c
8.	b	18.	b
9.	d	19.	b
10.	c	20.	a

CHAPTER 9: MOTIVATION

OUTLINE   (<u>S</u>urvey & <u>Q</u>uestion)

Use this outline when you survey the chapter, and enter your questions and comments in the space provided.

TOPIC	**NOTES**

I.   HUNGER AND EATING

    A.   Internal Factors:
        How Biology Affects
        Hunger

    B.   External Factors:
        How the Environment
        Affects Hunger

II.   SEXUAL MOTIVATION

    A.   Research Milestones:
        Kinsey, Masters and Johnson

B. Gender and Cultural
    Diversity: A Cultural
    Look at Sexual Behaviors

C. Sexual Behavior: Male/Female
    Variations and Similarities

D. Critical Thinking:
    Clarifying Your Sexual Values

E. Coercive Sex: Child
    Sexual Abuse, Sexual
    Harassment, and Rape

F. Gender and Cultural
    Diversity: Cultural
    Influences on Rape

III. ACHIEVEMENT MOTIVATION

A. Characteristics of Achievers:
    How Do They Differ?

B. <u>Gender</u> <u>and</u> <u>Cultural</u>
    <u>Diversity</u>: The Role of
    Diversity in Achievement

IV. THEORIES AND CONCEPTS

A. Biological Theories:
    Looking for Internal
    "Whys" of Behavior

B. Psychological Theories:
    The Role of Incentives
    and Cognitions

C. Maslow's Hierarchy of
    Needs: Combining Both
    Biological and Psychological
    Theories

LEARNING OBJECTIVES   (<u>R</u>ecite & w<u>R</u>ite)

Upon completion of Chapter 9, you should be able to:

1. Define <u>motivation</u>.

2. Describe the internal and external factors affecting the primary motive of hunger.

3. Describe the possible role of set points in obesity and discuss the three basic steps for successful weight management.

4. Define <u>anorexia</u> <u>nervosa</u> and <u>bulimia</u> and discuss their effects and possible causes.

5. Briefly describe sexual motivation and the contributions of Alfred Kinsey, William Masters and Virginia Johnson to our knowledge of human sexuality and the human sexual response.

6. Discuss the advantages of cultural studies in sex research.

7. Discuss the role of biology and learning on sexual arousal. Describe the power of sexual scripts and the role of the sympathetic and parasympathetic nervous systems in sexual response.

154

8. List and describe the four stages of Masters and Johnson's sexual response cycle.

9. Differentiate between a heterosexual, a bisexual, and a gay or lesbian.

10. Compare the biological and psychosocial models in their explanations for homosexuality.

11. Discuss the major causes of sexual problems.

12. Differentiate among child sexual abuse, pedophilia, and incest.

13. Discuss the three reasons why victims of child sexual abuse, sexual harassment, and rape are reluctant to report the assault.

14. Describe common myths about child sexual abuse and discuss the prime characteristics of the perpetrator.

15. Discuss four long-lasting effects of child sexual abuse and ways to prevent it.

16. Define _sexual_ _harassment_ and _rape_.

17. Discuss common myths about rape and the four prime motives. Describe the motivation for acquaintance rape.

18. Discuss the importance of culture on creating conditions conducive to rape.

19. Describe achievement motivation and the five characteristics of achievers.

20. Discuss how gender and culture might affect achievement. Explain the appeal of Horner's research on women's supposed "fear of success."

21. Describe the following biological theories of motivation: instinct theory, sociobiology, and drive-reduction theory.

156

22. Describe the following psychological theories of motivation:
    incentive theory, cognitive theories, and intrinsic versus
    extrinsic motivation.

23. Discuss Maslow's hierarchy of needs and explain how it
    combines both biological and psychological theories of
    motivation.

KEY TERMS   (Recite and wRite)

Upon completion of Chapter 9, you should be able to define the
following terms.

Achievement Motivation: _____

_____

AIDS (Acquired Immune Deficiency Syndrome): _____

_____

Anorexia Nervosa: _____

_____

Baseline: _____

_____

Bisexuality: _____

_____

Bulimia: _____

_____

Child Sexual Abuse: _____

_____

Drive-Reduction Theory: _____

_____

Ejaculation: _____

_____

Erectile Dysfunction: _____

_____

Erogenous Zones: _____

_____

Ethnocentrism: _____

_____

Ethology: _____

_____

Excitement Phase: _____

_____

Extrinsic Motivation: _____

_____

Heterosexuality: _____

_____

Hierarchy of Needs: _____

_____

Homophobia: _____

_____

Homosexuality: _____

_____

Incentive Theory: _____

_____

Incest: _____

_____

Instincts: _____

_____

Intrinsic Motivation: _____

_____

Lateral Hypothalamus (LH): _____

_____

Motivation: _____

_____

Orgasmic Dysfunction: _____

_____

Orgasm Phase: _____

_____

Pedophilia: _____

_____

Plateau Phase: _____

_____

Rape: _____

_____

Refractory Period: _____

_____

Resolution Phase: _____

_____

Set Point: _____

_____

Sexual Dysfunctions: _____

_____

Sexual Harassment: _____

_____

Sexual Orientation: _____

_____

Sexual Response Cycle: _____

_____

Sexual Scripts: _____

_____

Sociobiology: _____

_____

Ventromedial Hypothalamus (VMH): _____

_____

FILL-IN EXERCISES

Fill in the word or words that best fit in the spaces below.

1. _____ refers to internal factors that activate and direct behavior.

2. The _____ is the area of the brain that stimulates eating behaviors, whereas the _____ signals the organism to stop eating.

3. The eating disorder in which enormous quantities of food are consumed (binges), followed by purging by taking laxatives or vomiting is referred to as _____.

4. Masters and Johnson's four stages of the male and female physiological changes during sexual activity are known as the _____.

5. _____ is non-relative sexual gratification from contacts with children while _____ is sexual contact between two people who are related.

6. Unwelcome sexual advances, requests for sexual favors, and other unwelcome verbal or physical conduct of a sexual nature all represent what is known as _____.

7. The need for success, for doing better than others, and for mastering challenging tasks is referred to as _____.

8. According to _____ theory, motivation begins with a physiological need that elicits a psychological energy or drive directed toward behavior that will satisfy the original need.

9. _____ motivation is a desire to perform an activity because of external rewards or the avoidance of punishment. Motivation is not inherent in the behavior itself.

10. According to Maslow's _____, basic survival and security needs must be satisfied before one can move on to the higher needs such as self-actualization.

APPLICATION   (<u>R</u>ecite)

<u>Situation</u>

It is 11:30 a.m. and you are beginning to feel hungry. However, you are in the middle of doing something very important and you do not wish to stop just to eat. You guess that you can delay eating for a while longer, but soon your stomach begins to make noises and you realize you must eat. Besides, you are now really hungry and your work does not seem to flow as smoothly as it did before the hunger set in.

<u>Questions</u> <u>to</u> <u>Answer</u>

1. What are the physiological mechanisms that are creating your dilemma?

2. Why does your stomach make noise as you delay eating?

3. Might your work efficiency and productivity be affected because you are hungry?

4. What might happen to your work productivity once you have satisfied your need for food?

CRITICAL THINKING EXERCISE   (<u>R</u>ecite)

<u>Personal</u> <u>Values</u> <u>Clarification:</u> <u>Exploring</u> <u>Achievement</u> <u>Motivation</u> (An Affective Skill)

One of the most important ingredients of critical thinking is the ability to closely examine one's own <u>values</u> (ideals, mores, standards, and principles that guide behavior). Are the values you currently hold a simple reflection of the values of your family or peer group? Or are they the result of careful, deliberate choice? Have you listened carefully to opposing values and compared the relative costs and benefits? Since values have such a powerful influence on thinking, you should critically evaluate each of your personal values.

162

To help you explore your values, we offer several critical thinking questions regarding your own opinions about achievement motivation. While reading through the questions, jot your thoughts down and try to think of specific examples from your own experiences. You will find that sharing these written notes with others often leads to a fascinating discussion of how others perceive and define achievement motivation.

1. During your early childhood, did your parents encourage independent thinking? Did they allow you to do things on your own? Did they give you certain responsibilities and expect that you would carry them out?

2. During your early school years, did your parents help you with your homework? Did you want them to help you? Would you have preferred to have done the homework without their help?

3. In school, did you often raise your hand in response to a question by the teacher? Did you only raise your hand if you thought the question was challenging? Or did you raise your hand regardless of degree of difficulty?

4. When given an assignment in school, did you try to complete it in the easiest manner possible? Did you often try to supply more information than the teacher was seeking?

5. When given a choice of assignments by a teacher, did you usually choose the easiest? Did you choose the most challenging? Did you choose a task that fell somewhere in-between in terms of degree of difficulty?

6. In college, do you try to take the easiest courses? When you have to take a challenging course, do you try to get the easiest professor? Do you delay taking the course if the easiest professor is not teaching the class or the class was closed when you tried to register for it?

7. Do you delay taking the hardest courses in college until your last year? Do you delay all of the hardest courses or only some of them? If you delay taking the most challenging courses, why do you believe you are doing so?

8. Do you avoid taking the easiest courses in college? If so, why do you think you are doing so?

9. When you graduate from college, will you be going on for advanced training (e.g., graduate school, medical school, law school, etc.)? If not, why do you believe that one college degree is sufficient?

10. When you begin to look for a job, will you try to find one that requires a lot of work? Or will you look for an easy job? Or will you take any job that pays well? Will you seek a job that is challenging, or would you prefer not to be so challenged?

SAMPLE TEST QUESTIONS   (Review)

1. _____ activates, maintains, and directs behavior.

    a. Motivation
    b. An incentive
    c. A drive
    d. A need

2. This area of the hypothalamus is responsible for stimulation eating behavior.

    a. ventromedial hypothalamus (VMH)
    b. lateral hypothalamus (LH)
    c. medial hypothalamus (MH)
    d. bilateral hypothalamus (BH)

3. You have a friend who appears to have lost a lot of weight in a short period of time. You suspect she may be starving herself. After reading your psychology text, you think she might have the eating disorder of

    a. bulimia
    b. obesity
    c. anorexia nervosa
    d. gargantuaphobia

4. Viewing one's own ethnic group (or culture) as central and "correct" or "best", and then judging the rest of the world according to this standard is referred to as

   a. ethnicity
   b. prejudice
   c. cultural bias
   d. ethnocentrism

5. Homosexuality is believed to be caused by

   a. disturbed relationships with parents
   b. a hormonal imbalance before birth
   c. exploratory behavior with persons of the same sex at an early age
   d. unknown factors

6. Areas of the body that are particularly sensitive to touch and sexual arousal are known as

   a. erectile tissues
   b. erogenous zones
   c. primary sex characteristics
   d. high libido zones

7. Orgasm refers to

   a. the final phase of the sexual response cycle
   b. the male refractory period
   c. the point at which the individual experiences a highly intense and pleasurable sense of release of tension
   d. a living entity

8. During this phase of the sexual response, the body returns to its unaroused state.

   a. resolution phase
   b. plateau phase
   c. refractory phase
   d. excitatory phase

9. A sexual orientation that includes both same sex and other sex partners is

   a. homosexuality
   b. bisexuality
   c. heterosexuality
   d. transexuality

10. This sexually transmitted disease attacks the body's immune system.

    a. syphilis
    b. gonorrhea
    c. AIDS
    d. herpes

11. One of the earliest and most extensive surveys of human sexual behavior in the United States was conducted by

    a. Abraham Maslow
    b. William Masters and Virginia Johnson
    c. Martin Weinberg
    d. Alfred Kinsey

12. The irrational fear of homosexuality is referred to as

    a. biphobia
    b. homophobia
    c. heterophobia
    d. transphobia

13. An adult engaging in sexual contact of any kind with a child, including indecent exposure, inappropriate touching, oral-genital stimulation, masturbation, and anal and/or vaginal intercourse is referred to as

    a. pedophilia
    b. incest
    c. child sexual abuse
    d. rape

14. Sexual gratification from contacts with children who are not relatives is referred to as

    a. pedophilia
    b. incest
    c. rape
    d. gratifilia

15. All but one of the following may be considered forms of sexual harassment.

    a. unwelcome sexual advances
    b. requests for sexual favors
    c. smiling at someone
    d. unwelcome verbal conduct of a sexual nature

16. This branch of biology is concerned with studying animal behavior under natural conditions.

    a. ethnology
    b. sociobiology
    c. ethology
    d. ethnicity

17. According to the drive-reduction theory, motivation begins with a

    a. goal
    b. physiological need
    c. cognitive need
    d. motivational need

18. The incentive theory of motivation emphasizes the importance of _____ in creating behavior.

    a. homeostasis
    b. biological needs
    c. external stimuli
    d. "push" mechanisms that result from deprivation

19. Research with intrinsic versus extrinsic motivation finds that when one receives extrinsic rewards, interest and motivation

    a. decline
    b. increase
    c. stay the same
    d. it depends on the situation

20. The psychologist associated with a hierarchy of needs is

    a. Murray
    b. Freud
    c. Skinner
    d. Maslow

ANSWERS

FILL-IN EXERCISES

1. Motivation   2. lateral hypothalamus, ventromedial hypothalamus   3. bulimia   4. sexual response cycle
5. Pedophilia, incest   6. sexual harassment   7. achievement motivation   8. drive-reduction   9. Extrinsic   10. hierarchy of needs

SAMPLE TEST QUESTIONS

1.	a	11.	d
2.	b	12.	b
3.	c	13.	c
4.	d	14.	a
5.	d	15.	c
6.	b	16.	c
7.	c	17.	b
8.	a	18.	c
9.	b	19.	a
10.	c	20.	d

CHAPTER 10: EMOTION, STRESS, AND COPING

OUTLINE (<u>S</u>urvey & <u>Q</u>uestion)

Use this outline when you survey the chapter, and enter your questions and comments in the space provided.

TOPIC   **NOTES**

I. UNDERSTANDING EMOTION

    A. The Study of Emotions: How Scientists Study Feelings

    B. The Biology of Emotions: The Role of the Brain and Autonomic Nervous System

    C. <u>Gender</u> <u>and</u> <u>Cultural</u> <u>Diversity</u>: Evolutionary and Cultural Influences on Emotion

II. GENERAL THEORIES OF EMOTION

A. James-Lange Theory:
The Reaction <u>Is</u> the
Emotion

B. Cannon-Bard Theory:
Emotions and Reactions are
Simultaneous

C. Facial Feedback Hypothesis:
The Face Determines Emotions

D. Cognitive Labeling Theory:
The Label Is the Emotion

III. STRESS

A. Causes of Stress: From Major
Life Changes to Minor Hassles

B. <u>Critical</u> <u>Thinking</u>:
Recognizing the Role of Personal
Values in Conflict Resolution

C. Results of Stress:
   How the Body Responds

D. Stress and Cardiovascular Disorders:
   The Leading Cause of Death in the
   United States

IV. COPING WITH STRESS

A. Emotion-Focused Forms
   of Coping: Reappraising
   the Situation

B. Problem-Focused Forms
   of Coping: Putting
   Problem-Solving Skills
   to Work

C. Resources for Effective
   Coping: From Good Health
   to Money

D. Specific Coping Strategies:
   How You Can Reduce Stress

LEARNING OBJECTIVES   (<u>R</u>ecite & w<u>R</u>ite)

Upon completion of Chapter 10, you should be able to:

1. Define <u>emotion</u> and <u>stress</u>.

2. Explain what is meant by the cognitive, subjective, behavioral, and physiological components of emotion.

3. Describe how scientists use self-report techniques to measure the cognitive and subjective components and the polygraph to measure the physiological component. Discuss the research concerning effectiveness of the polygraph as a lie detector.

4. Explain how the limbic system of the brain and the sympathetic and parasympathetic branches of the autonomic nervous system (ANS) work during emotional arousal.

5. Discuss evolutionary and cultural influences on emotion.

6. Compare and contrast the James-Lange, Cannon-Bard, facial feedback, and cognitive labeling theories of emotion.

172

7. Discuss the role of misattribution in emotion.

8. Describe a stressor. Distinguish between eustress and distress.

9. Discuss the following causes of stress and relevant criticisms: life changes, poor working conditions or bad family life, hassles, frustrations, and conflicts.

10. Describe the physiological effects of stress, including the effects of stress on the immune system.

11. Explain the relationship of the cardiovascular disorders, hypertension and heart disease, to stress.

12. Discuss the difference between a Type-A and a Type-B personality and tell why a Type-A is more at risk for cardiovascular disorders.

13. Discuss both emotion-focused and problem-focused forms of coping with stress.

14. List and discuss the different resources for effective coping with stress.

15. Describe the influence of relaxation and exercise in reducing stress.

KEY TERMS (Recite and wRite)

Upon completion of Chapter 10, you should be able to define the following terms.

Approach-Approach Conflict: _____

_____

Approach-Avoidance Conflict: _____

_____

Avoidance-Avoidance Conflict: _____

_____

Cannon-Bard Theory: _____

_____

Cognitive Labeling Theory: _____

_____

Conflict: _____

_____

Coping: _____

_____

Emotion: _____

_____

Emotion-Focused Forms of Coping: _____

_____

Epinephrine: _____

_____

Essential Hypertension: _____

_____

Facial Feedback Hypothesis: _____

_____

Frustration: _____

_____

General Adaptation Syndrome: _____

_____

Heart Disease: _____

_____

Hypertension: _____

_____

Internal Locus of Control: _____

_____

James-Lange Theory: _____

_____

Misattribution: _____

_____

Parasympathetic Nervous System: _____

_____

Polygraph: _____

_____

Problem-Focused Forms of Coping: _____

_____

Relaxation Techniques: _____

_____

Stress: _____

_____

Stressor: _____

_____

Sympathetic Nervous System: _____

_____

Type-A Personality: _____

_____

Type-B Personality: _____

_____

FILL-IN EXERCISES   (Review & wRite)

Fill in the word or words that best fit in the spaces below.

1.   _____ refers to feelings or affective responses that result from physiological arousal, thoughts and beliefs, subjective evaluation, and bodily expression.

2.   The four basic components of emotions include the _____, _____, _____, and _____.

3.   According to the _____ theory of emotions, the physiological arousal precedes experiencing of the emotion, whereas the _____ theory suggests that emotions result from simultaneous stimulation of the cortex and the autonomic nervous system.

4.   Proponents of the _____ theory believe that emotions result from a combination of the subjective, cognitive, and physiological arousal components of emotion.

5.   The part of the autonomic nervous system that is activated under stressful conditions is the _____ nervous system.

6.   Infant and cross-cultural similarities in emotional expression support the _____ theory of emotions first advanced by Charles Darwin.

7.   An _____ conflict is one in which a person must choose between two or more alternatives that will both lead to undesirable results.

8.   The three-phase bodily response to chronic stress that includes the alarm reaction, the phase of resistance, and the stage of exhaustion is the _____.

9.   People who are ambitious, competitive, and hurried may have a _____ personality; people who have a laid-back, calm, relaxed attitude are considered to have a _____ personality.

10. The two major forms of coping with stress are _____ and _____.

APPLICATION   (Recite)

Situation

You remember that when you were a student in the elementary grades, you had difficulty taking tests because they made you very nervous. You realized that as you grew older, this nervousness was really something called stress. In college, there have been situations where you studied very hard for an exam. However, upon taking the exam, your mind seemed to go blank. You know you studied very hard, but somehow the information stored in your brain could not be retrieved.

Questions to Answer

  1. How could you recognize that stress was the cause of your problem during an exam instead of simply not sufficiently preparing?

  2. What are some methods that could be used to help you deal with your stress?

  3. If the stress is left untreated, could this lead to something more serious? Give examples.

  4. Is stress coping related to any personality factors?

CRITICAL THINKING EXERCISE   (Recite)

Developing Self-Understanding (An Affective Skill)

When critical thinkers master a new skill or discover an insight, they are able to transfer this information to new contexts. Noncritical thinkers can often provide correct answers, repeat definitions, and carry out formulae, yet remain unable to transfer their knowledge to new situations because of a basic lack of understanding.

For each of the following situations, using your critical thinking skills, give an example of an emotion-focused and a problem-focused form of coping. In the case of emotion-focused coping strategies, describe a change in view or a reappraisal of the stressful situation. For problem-focused coping strategies, describe how you could deal directly with the stressor in ways that would decrease or eliminate it.

1. One of your coworkers avoids you and describes you in unfavorable ways to others.

    Emotion-focused: _____

    Problem-focused: _____

2. You are getting a below-average grade in your chemistry class.

    Emotion-focused: _____

    Problem-focused: _____

3. You lost your job when the store in which you worked closed down.

    Emotion-focused: _____

    Problem-focused: _____

4. The person you love has started acting distant.

    Emotion-focused: _____

    Problem-focused: _____

5. You have just discovered that one of your children needs a liver transplant.

    Emotion-focused: _____

    Problem-focused: _____

SAMPLE TEST QUESTIONS   (<u>R</u>eview)

1. The _____ component of emotions involves active changes in the body, such as pupil dilation or increased heart rate.

    a. cognitive
    b. psychological
    c. physiological
    d. behavioral

2. The apparatus commonly used as a "lie detector" is called a(n)

   a. electroencephalograph
   b. EEG
   c. polygraph
   d. galvanograph

3. You suddenly see an oncoming car in your lane. You swerve to miss it, and your car finally comes to a bouncing halt in the ditch at the side of the road. At this point you notice your high level of fear. This reaction best supports the _____ theory of emotions.

   a. Cannon-Bard
   b. James-Lange
   c. cognitive labeling
   d. common sense

4. You are kissing your dating partner good night and you notice that you are physiologically aroused. You think about your feelings and decide that you are probably in love with this individual. Your response best supports the _____ theory of emotions.

   a. Cannon-Bard
   b. James-Lange
   c. cognitive labeling
   d. companionate love

5. The theory that stresses that an individual's interpretation or label for physiological arousal determines the emotion experienced is

   a. Cannon-Bard
   b. James-Lange
   c. cognitive labeling
   d. arousal

6. The facial feedback hypothesis proposes that
   a. movements of the facial muscles produce emotional reactions
   b. mood swings are triggered by facial ticks
   c. lies can be detected by facial expression changes
   d. information reception can be detected in facial movements

7. Misattribution is when

   a. a person mistakenly believes the cause of an emotion is something other than it really is
   b. a person correctly interprets an emotion
   c. a person misconstrues one emotion for another
   d. a person realizes that arousal has overtaken responding

8. Hans Selye defines stress as

   a. the reaction of the autonomic nervous system to a specific challenge imposed from outside the body
   b. the nonspecific response of the body to any demand made on it
   c. any situation that causes activation of the sympathetic nervous system
   d. the intellectual response made to any stressor

9. A stressor is

   a. a stimulus that causes stress
   b. relative to only one culture and everyone within that culture will experience the same stressors
   c. roughly equivalent to punishment
   d. anything that causes bad things to happen

10. The three phases of the general adaptation syndrome are

    a. preparation, alarm reaction, incubation
    b. alarm reaction, incubation, resistance
    c. alarm reaction, resistance, exhaustion
    d. incubation, resistance, exhaustion

11. Stress can

    a. strengthen heart muscle
    b. suppress the release of glucose into the bloodstream
    c. cause brain cells to multiply
    d. improve body metabolism

12. Which of the following is one of the ways stress might contribute to cancer?

    a. reducing the amount of glucose in the bloodstream
    b. suppressing the immune system
    c. making more interferon available
    d. increasing the metabolism of cancer cells

13. The Type-A behavior pattern is associated with

    a. chronic pain
    b. cancer
    c. smoking cigarettes
    d. heart disease

14. Essential hypertension is

    a. a disorder of the heart muscle
    b. a major cause of cancer in males
    c. elevated blood pressure with no related medical cause
    d. elevated blood pressure because of kidney failure

15. Slow normal speech, relaxed and comfortable posture, and a
    good sense of humor are characteristics of

    a. brain disease
    b. Type-A behavior
    c. Type-B behavior
    d. Alzheimer's disease

16. Many psychological defense mechanisms are examples of

    a. emotion-focused forms of coping with stress
    b. psychosis
    c. problem-focused forms of coping with stress
    d. hassles

17. Which of the following is a good resource for effective
    coping with stress?

    a. positive beliefs
    b. alcohol
    c. social isolation
    d. increased eating

18. Trying to decide which of two equally good concerts to
    attend on a Friday night is a(n)

    a. approach-avoidance conflict
    b. avoidance-avoidance conflict
    c. approach-approach conflict
    d. transitory positive conflict

182

19. When undergoing any stress, your body undergoes several
     major and minor changes. The most significant are those
     controlled by the

     a. somatic nervous system
     b. spinal cord
     c. hippocampus
     d. autonomic nervous system

20. Life changes may affect health because they

     a. increase the number of hassles
     b. cause us to reassess our life style
     c. are always the result of something bad happening
     d. are known to increase the level of cortisol above normal

ANSWERS

<u>FILL-IN</u> <u>EXERCISES</u>

1. Emotion   2. physiological, cognitive, behavioral,
subjective experience 3. James-Lange, Cannon-Bard
4. cognitive labeling   5. sympathetic   6. evolutionary
7. avoidance-avoidance 8. General Adaptation Syndrome
9.   Type-A, Type-B 10. emotion-focused, problem-focused

<u>SAMPLE</u> <u>TEST</u> <u>QUESTIONS</u>

1.	c	11.	b
2.	c	12.	b
3.	b	13.	d
4.	c	14.	c
5.	c	15.	c
6.	a	16.	a
7.	a	17.	a
8.	b	18.	c
9.	a	19.	d
10.	c	20.	a

184

CHAPTER 11: PERSONALITY

OUTLINE   (<u>S</u>urvey & <u>Q</u>uestion)

Use this outline when you survey the chapter, and enter your questions and comments in the space provided.

| **TOPIC** | **NOTES** |

I.   DISPOSITIONAL THEORIES

A.   Type Theories: The
     "Discrete Categories"
     View of Personality

B.   Trait Theories: The
     "Continuum" Approach to
     Personality

C.   Evaluating Type and Trait
     Theories: Three Major
     Criticisms

II. PSYCHOANALYTIC THEORIES

A. Freud's Psychoanalytic Theory: The Power of the Unconscious

B. Neo-Freudian Theories: Revising Freud's Ideas

C. <u>Gender</u> <u>and</u> <u>Cultural</u> <u>Diversity</u>: Horney, Freud, and Penis Envy

D. Evaluating Psychoanalytic Theories: Four Areas of Criticism

III. LEARNING THEORIES

A. Behavioral Perspectives: Watson's and Skinner's Contributions

B. Social Learning Theory: The Power of Observation and Imitation

C. Evaluating Learning Theories:
Admirers Versus Critics

IV. HUMANISTIC THEORIES

A. Carl Rogers: The Self-Concept
Theory of Personality

B. Abraham Maslow: The Search
for Self-Actualization

C. Evaluating Humanistic Theories:
Three Major Criticisms

V. OTHER APPROACHES TO PERSONALITY

A. Cognitive Perspectives:
Bandura's and Rotter's
Contributions

B. Biological Theories:
A Genetic Approach to
Personality

     E.   <u>Gender</u> <u>and</u> <u>Cultural</u>
          <u>Diversity</u>: Cultural
          Concepts of "Self"

     F.   <u>Critical</u> <u>Thinking</u>:
          Popularized Personality
          Tests

LEARNING OBJECTIVES   (<u>R</u>ecite & w<u>R</u>ite)

After reading Chapter 11, you should be able to:

1. Define <u>personality</u> and explain the difficulty with its
    definition.

2. Discuss type theories of personality and explain Sheldon's
    somatotype theory.

3. Discuss trait theories and describe the theories developed
    by the following individuals: Allport, Cattell, and
    Eysenck. Explain the "Big 5" model of personality.

4. Discuss the three major criticisms of type and trait
    theories.

5. Describe how psychoanalytic theory differs from type and trait theories.

6. Differentiate among Freud's three levels of consciousness: conscious, preconscious, and unconscious.

7. Explain Freud's three mental structures that make up personality: id, ego, and superego. Discuss how the pleasure principle, reality principle, and morality principle correspond to each of these structures. Explain the role of defense mechanisms.

8. Discuss Freud's five stages of psychosexual development and their effect on adult personality.

9. Compare the neo-Freudian approach to personality development with Freud's views. Differentiate among the theories of Adler, Jung, and Horney.

10. Discuss the four major criticisms of psychoanalytic theories.

11. Discuss the learning theory approach to explaining personality. Compare the behaviorist approach of Watson and Skinner to social-learning theory.

12. Evaluate the criticism of learning theory.

13. Discuss the humanistic approach to personality. Compare the theories of Carl Rogers and Abraham Maslow.

14. Discuss the three major criticisms of humanistic theories.

15. Discuss the cognitive approach to personality. Compare the theories of Albert Bandura and Julian Rotter.

16. Explain the biological approach to personality and discuss the research regarding shyness as an inherited trait.

17. Describe the usefulness of interactionism in combining the best elements of each theory of personality.

18. Discuss why modern methods of personality assessment are better than ancient models such as phrenology; include the terms of reliability and validity.

19. Explain the use of interviews and observation in personality assessment.

20. Describe the use of objective tests such as the MMPI in personality assessment.

21. Compare projective tests with objective personality measurement approaches. Describe the Rorschach and the Thematic Apperception Test (TAT).

22. Discuss the three major criticisms concerning personality assessment.

23. Describe cultural variations in the emphasis on "self" and discuss how these affect the study of personality.

KEY TERMS   (<u>R</u>ecite & w<u>R</u>ite)

Upon completion of Chapter 11, you should be able to define the following terms.

Anal Stage: _____

_____

Archetypes: _____

_____

Basic Anxiety: _____

_____

Cardinal Traits: _____

_____

Central Traits: _____

_____

Collective Unconscious: _____

_____

Conscious: _____

_____

Defense Mechanisms: _____

_____

Ego: _____

_____

Electra Complex: _____

_____

Factor Analysis: _____

_____

Genital Stage: _____

_____

Hysterical Neurosis: _____

_____

Id: _____

_____

Inferiority Complex: _____

_____

Latency Stage: _____

_____

Locus of Control: _____

_____

Neo-Freudians: _____

_____

Oedipus Complex: _____

_____

194

Oral Stage: _____

_____

Personality: _____

_____

Phallic Stage: _____

_____

Phenomenological Perspective: _____

_____

Phrenology: _____

_____

Pleasure Principle: _____

_____

Preconscious: _____

_____

Projective Tests: _____

_____

Psychosexual Stages: _____

_____

Reality Principle: _____

_____

Reciprocal Determinism: _____

_____

Repression: _____

_____

Rorschach Inkblot Test: _____

_____

Secondary Traits: _____

_____

Self-Actualization: _____

_____

Self-Concept: _____

_____

Self-Efficacy: _____

_____

Self-Esteem: _____

_____

Social Learning Theory: _____

_____

Source Traits: _____

_____

Superego: _____

_____

Thematic Apperception Test (TAT): _____

_____

196

Trait: _____

_____

Unconditional Positive Regard: _____

_____

Unconscious: _____

_____

FILL-IN EXERCISES   (<u>R</u>eview & w<u>R</u>ite)

Fill in the word or words that best fit in the spaces below.

1. _____ theories of personality divide people into discrete categories based on prominent, consistent behavioral characteristics; _____ theories of personality suggest that people can vary in their personality characteristics along a wide range of values.

2. Allport referred to characteristics that dominate a person's life as _____ traits, and he called each individual's specific, highly characteristic qualities _____ traits.

3. Freud's developmental theory of personality is known as _____ or _____ theory.

4. The superego contains the _____ and the _____ which provide moral judgments for the ego.

5. Repression is an example of a _____ used to escape or avoid anxiety.

6. Horney suggested the term _____ envy be replaced by _____ envy. She also countered that some men develop _____ envy--the desire to bear and nurse children.

7. Learning theories include _____ and _____ approaches that focus on conditioning and observational learning.

8. Maslow's belief that all people are motivated toward personal growth and development is known as _____.

9. _____ tests measure potential abilities, while _____ tests measure what you have already learned.

10. The Rorschach inkblot test and the Thematic Apperception Test are _____ tests that use neutral or ambiguous stimulus materials.

APPLICATION   (Recite)

Situation

A friend of yours used to suck his thumb when he was a little boy. When he became an adult, he starting overeating and smoking cigarettes. He realizes that overeating and smoking are bad and unhealthy habits, but he cannot stop. He has tried a variety of treatment techniques, but none seems to work.

Questions to Answer

1. What labels and characteristics would psychoanalytic theory attach to your friend?

2. What suggestions would psychoanalytic theory offer to help your friend?

3. How would a behavior or learning therapist interpret your friend's problem? What suggestions for treatment might she make?

4. What might a cognitive approach offer to your friend's inability to deal with his habits?

CRITICAL THINKING EXERCISE (<u>R</u>ecite)

<u>Employing</u> <u>Precise</u> <u>Terms:</u>   <u>Defense</u> <u>Mechanisms</u>
   (A Behavioral Skill)

A critical thinker is capable of reading a description of an event and determining if this event matches a given situation or individual. Often events are not easily described, but a critical thinker can analyze a situation and often determine which of a number of events best describes it. Thus, if presented with a number of behavioral descriptions of an individual, such as defense mechanisms, the critical thinker should be able to determine which mechanism best applies in a given situation.

By Freud's definition, defense mechanisms operate at the unconscious level; therefore, according to Freud, we are not aware when we are using them. If, however, we can easily observe the use of defense mechanisms in others from their excessive or inappropriate behaviors, we may be able to identify when we ourselves use them. By doing this, we are in a better position of being able to replace inappropriate behaviors with more beneficial problem-solving approaches.

Apply your behavioral, critical thinking skill and try to identify the type of defense mechanisms being used by the people described in the following examples (answers are at the back of this chapter), and see if you can identify when you or others in the real world use defense mechanisms.

   1. A woman who was assaulted and raped several years ago in a terrifying attack has forgotten the incident.

_____

   2. Luis told his fiancee Susan about his prior sexual involvement with other women but Susan has no recollection of the conversation.

_____

3. Laleh has just read an article describing danger signals indicating skin cancer. She examines the marks on her face and discusses the tendency for her family members to have freckles and moles with irregular borders.

_____

4. Matt received a notice that he has been put on academic probation. Since he will not be able to play football during the coming semester if he is on probation, he decided to leave college and said he wants to spend his time doing something "worthwhile."

_____

5. An anonymous person wrote a letter to the editor of a newspaper claiming that police officers do not treat their trained dogs properly. He or she claimed to be an animal lover who feels that anyone mistreating animals should be tortured.

_____

SAMPLE TEST QUESTIONS   (Review)

1. According to Allport, _____ traits are characteristics such as ambition or humility that organize a person's life.

    a. common
    b. unique
    c. cardinal
    d. central

2. According to Cattell, there are 16 basic personality dimensions, which he calls _____ traits.

    a. cardinal
    b. central
    c. source
    d. secondary

3. According to Sheldon, a(n) _____ has a dominant gastrointestinal system and is overweight.

   a. ectomorph
   b. endomorph
   c. mesomorph
   d. astromorph

4. According to Freudian theory, the _____ is the part of the psyche that provides instinctual motivation for behavior.

   a. id
   b. superego
   c. ego
   d. ego-ideal

5. Freud's most important defense mechanism that involves unconscious blocking of unacceptable impulses to keep them from awareness is referred to as

   a. repression
   b. regression
   c. projection
   d. reaction formation

6. This stage of psychosexual development begins in puberty and represents mature adult sexuality and personality development.

   a. oral stage
   b. anal stage
   c. phallic stage
   d. genital stage

7. Compared with Freudian theory, neo-Freudian approaches tend to emphasize the

   a. importance of the superego
   b. unconscious mind
   c. impact of social and cultural influences
   d. importance of sexual impulses

8. The concept of "will to power" that causes children to strive to be superior to others and develop their own capacities was formulated by

    a. Freud
    b. Erikson
    c. Adler
    d. Jung

9. The collective unconscious contains

    a. a personal unconscious
    b. the conscience
    c. the ego-ideal
    d. archetypes

10. Learning theory emphasizes the importance of

    a. the environment or situation
    b. unconscious impulses
    c. the reasoning process
    d. the self-concept

11. Social learning theory emphasizes the importance of

    a. operant conditioning
    b. classical conditioning
    c. role models
    d. unconscious impulses

12. Humanistic approaches to personality emphasize the importance of

    a. intrapsychic conflicts
    b. archetypes
    c. observational learning
    d. self-actualization

13. Humanistic approaches to personality are sometimes referred to collectively as the

    a. psychoanalytic perspective
    b. phenomenological perspective
    c. learning perspective
    d. behaviorist perspective

14. According to Carl Rogers, it is important to receive unconditional positive regard in order to develop a(n) _____ that is capable of self-actualization.

    a. psyche
    b. personal unconscious
    c. ego
    d. self-concept

15. The cognitive approach to personality is most likely to analyze

    a. self-fulfilling prophesies
    b. self-talk
    c. conditions of worth
    d. archetypes

16. Julian Rotter's theory is similar to Bandura's in suggesting that learning creates cognitive _____ that guide behavior and influence the environment.

    a. confusions
    b. frustrations
    c. confirmations
    d. expectancies

17. The MMPI is an example of a(n)

    a. projective test
    b. interview
    c. objective test
    d. rating scale

18. The _____ is a widely used self-report test that determines the presence of disturbed personality characteristics.

    a. 16 PF
    b. MMPI
    c. Internal-External Locus of Control Test
    d. structured interview

19. Which of the following is a projective test?

    a. 16 PF
    b. MMPI
    c. TAT
    d. Internal-External Locus of Control Test

20. The Rorschach tests a person's responses to

    a. pictures
    b. movies
    c. sentences
    d. inkblots

ANSWERS

FILL-IN EXERCISES

1. Type, trait   2. cardinal, central   3. psychoanalytic,
psychodynamic   4. conscience, ego-ideal   5. defense
mechanism   6. penis, power, womb   7. behaviorist, social
learning 8. self-actualization   9. Aptitude, achievement
10. projective

CRITICAL THINKING EXERCISE

1. repression   2. repression   3. intellectualization
4. rationalization   5. reaction formation

SAMPLE TEST QUESTIONS

1.	c	11.	c
2.	c	12.	d
3.	b	13.	b
4.	a	14.	d
5.	a	15.	b
6.	d	16.	d
7.	c	17.	c
8.	c	18.	b
9.	d	19.	c
10.	a	20.	d

CHAPTER 12: ABNORMAL BEHAVIOR

OUTLINE   (<u>S</u>urvey & <u>Q</u>uestion)

Use this outline when you survey the chapter, and enter your questions and comments in the space provided.

TOPIC	**NOTES**

I.   STUDYING ABNORMAL BEHAVIOR

A.   Identifying Abnormal
     Behavior: Three Standards

B.   <u>Gender</u> <u>and</u> <u>Cultural</u>
     <u>Diversity</u>: Culture
     and Mental Health

C.   Explaining Abnormality:
     From Superstition to
     Science

D.   Classifying Abnormal
     Behaviors: The Diagnostic
     and Statistical Manual IV

II. ANXIETY DISORDERS

206

A. Unreasonable Anxiety:
Five Major Anxiety
Disorders

B. Causes of Anxiety Disorders:
Learning or Biology?

III. SCHIZOPHRENIA

A. Symptoms of Schizophrenia:
Disturbances in Perception,
Language and Thought, Affect,
and Behavior

B. Subtypes of Schizophrenia:
Recent Methods of
Classification

C. Causes of Schizophrenia:
Nature and Nurture
Theories

D. Gender and Cultural
Diversity: Culture
and Schizophrenia

IV. MOOD DISORDERS

    A. Understanding Mood
        Disorders: Major
        Depressive Disorder
        and Bipolar Disorder

    B. Causes of Mood Disorders:
        Biological Versus
        Psychological Factors

    C. <u>Gender</u> <u>and</u> <u>Cultural</u>
        <u>Diversity</u>: Gender,
        Culture, and Depression

    D. Suicide: Ending
        Your Own Life

V. OTHER DISORDERS

    A. Dissociative Disorders:
        When the Personality
        Splits Apart

B. Somatoform Disorders:
    Psychological Disorders
    and the Body

C. <u>Gender</u> <u>and</u> <u>Cultural</u>
    <u>Diversity</u>: Hysteria
    and the "Wandering Uterus"

D. Personality Disorders:
    The Antisocial Personality

E. Substance Related
    Disorder: When Does
    Drug Use Become Abnormal?

VI. PROBLEMS WITH DIAGNOSIS
    AND LABELING

A. <u>Critical</u> <u>Thinking</u>:
    Do Diagnostic Labels of
    Mental Disorders Help or
    Hinder Effective Treatment?

LEARNING OBJECTIVES   (Recite & wRite)

Upon completion of Chapter 12, you should be able to:

1. Discuss the three standards for defining abnormal behavior:
    statistical, subjective discomfort, and maladaptive
    functioning approaches. Describe the limits of each
    approach.

2. Explain why windigo psychosis is considered to be a
    culturally relative disorder rather than a culturally
    universal disorder.

3. Summarize the history of explanations for abnormal behavior,
    including the demonological model, the medical model,
    exorcism, and asylums. In reference to modern times,
    discuss the influence of the medical model and Szasz's
    criticism of the label "mentally ill."

4. Describe the DSM-IV system used to classify psychological
    disorders, give reasons for changes from earlier editions,
    and identify myths and appropriate evidence regarding those
    who are considered abnormal.

5. Describe the five major anxiety disorders and discuss their
    possible causes.

6. Define <u>schizophrenia</u> and describe the four major symptoms that are characteristic of schizophrenia. Discuss the proposed classification system according to positive and negative symptoms of schizophrenia.

7. Compare the biological and psychosocial theories of possible causes of schizophrenia and discuss the criticism of these theories.

8. Discuss the four major ways schizophrenia differs across cultures.

9. Compare major depressive disorder with bipolar disorder and discuss biological and psychological explanations for their possible causes.

10. Describe the similarities and differences in depression across cultures and explain why women are more likely to be depressed.

11. Discuss the problem of suicide and how to tell if someone is suicidal.

12. Discuss the major feature of dissociative disorders and summarize the characteristics of dissociative amnesia, dissociative fugue, and multiple personality disorder.

13. Describe the nature of somatoform disorders and how conversion disorder differs from hypochondriasis.

14. Discuss why the early Greeks thought hysteria was caused by a wandering uterus.

15. Define personality disorders and discuss the major symptoms and possible causes of antisocial personality disorder.

16. Describe substance related disorders and differentiate between substance abuse and substance dependence. Explain why alcohol is our major drug problem and discuss the theories that attempt to explain alcoholism.

17. Describe Rosenhan's study with "pseudopatients" and how it relates to problems with diagnosing and labeling abnormal behaviors.

212

KEY TERMS   (<u>R</u>ecite and w<u>R</u>ite)

Upon completion of Chapter 12, you should be able to define the following terms.

Abnormal Behavior: _____

_____

Antisocial Personality: _____

_____

Anxiety Disorders: _____

_____

Bipolar Disorder: _____

_____

Catalepsy: _____

_____

Conversion Disorder: _____

_____

Delusions: _____

_____

Diagnostic and Statistical Manual of Mental Disorders (DSM-IV):

_____

_____

Dissociative Amnesia: _____

_____

Dissociative Fugue: _____

_____

Dissociative Disorders: _____

_____

Dopamine Hypothesis: _____

_____

Egocentrism: _____

_____

Generalized Anxiety Disorder: _____

_____

Hallucinations: _____

_____

Hypochondriasis: _____

_____

Insanity: _____

_____

Learned Helplessness: _____

_____

Major Depressive Disorder: _____

_____

Maladaptive Functioning Standard: _____

_____

214

Medical Model: _____

_____

Multiple Personality Disorder (MPD): _____

_____

Neurosis: _____

_____

Obsessive-Compulsive Disorder (OCD): _____

_____

Panic Disorders: _____

_____

Paranoia: _____

_____

Personality Disorders: _____

_____

Phobia: _____

_____

Posttraumatic Stress Disorder (PTSD): _____

_____

Psychiatry: _____

_____

Psychosis: _____

_____

Schizophrenia: _____

_____

Somatoform Disorder: _____

_____

Statistical Standard: _____

_____

Subjective Discomfort Standard: _____

_____

Substance Related Disorders: _____

_____

Substance Abuse: _____

_____

Substance Dependence: _____

_____

Trephining: _____

_____

Two-Syndrome Hypothesis: _____

_____

Waxy Flexibility: _____

_____

FILL-IN EXERCISES   (Review & wRite)

Fill in the word or words that best fit in the spaces below.

1. The _____ replaced a belief in demons or witchcraft with the assumption that abnormal behaviors were "mental illnesses."

2. A major difference between psychosis and neurosis is that in _____ there is a major loss of contact with reality.

3. _____ are anxiety disorders with exaggerated irrational fears of specific objects or situations.

4. In _____ disorders, there are anxiety-arousing thoughts and ritualistic behaviors.

5. In _____ stress disorder, the person has experienced an overwhelming stress.

6. Schizophrenic symptoms have been related to increased activity of _____ neurotransmitter circuits.

7. The two major types of mood disorders are _____ and _____.

8. Martin Seligman has suggested that individuals who believe they are unable to control or escape from sources of pain and sadness may develop _____.

9. Use of a psychoactive drug is classified as substance _____ when it interferes with social and occupational functioning and causes tolerance and withdrawal symptoms.

10. Failure of hospital staff to detect fake patients in David Rosenhan's study can be attributed to the effects of _____.

APPLICATION   (Recite)

Situation

A friend of yours has been feeling pretty depressed. He just
failed his first exam in college and he cannot seem to get over
this disappointment. Not only is he upset but he is afraid to
tell his parents of his failure. He never failed a test in his
life and he cannot understand what has happened to him. After
this failure experience, he isolated himself from others for a
number of days. However, when he was invited to a party, he
decided this would be good for him and so he accepted the offer.

Questions to Answer

  1.   Does your friend appear to have symptoms that might be
       described as abnormal?

  2.   What symptoms would be required for your friend to exhibit
       the abnormal forms of depression discussed in Chapter 12?

  3.   Does it appear that your friend may need some professional
       help in dealing with his depression?

  4.   Can you think of any situation in which you experienced
       depression? How did you deal with this depression?

CRITICAL THINKING EXERCISE   (Recite)

Distinguishing Fact From Opinion   (A Behavioral Skill)

When thinking critically about controversial issues, it is
helpful to make a distinction between statements of fact and
statements of opinion. (A fact is a statement that can be proven
true. An opinion is a statement that expresses how a person
feels about an issue or what someone thinks is true.) Although
it is also important to later determine whether the facts are
true or false, in this exercise simply mark "O" for opinion and
"F" for fact. After you have responded to each of the items, you
may wish to discuss your answers with your friends and
classmates.

218

_____ 1. The mentally ill are more dangerous than the general
            public.

_____ 2. The insanity plea allows criminals back on the street
            too soon.

_____ 3. Individuals who are diagnosed as having a "split
            personality" are also known as schizophrenics.

_____ 4. People who talk to themselves are probably
            schizophrenics.

_____ 5. Everyone has a behavioral disorder of one type or
            another.

_____ 6. Delusions and hallucinations are basically one in the
            same.

_____ 7. Individuals who are compulsive about keeping their
            rooms clean probably suffer from an obsessive-
            compulsive disorder.

_____ 8. Any form of depression is considered abnormal and
            likely requires professional treatment.

_____ 9. Posttraumatic stress as a disorder is the invention
            of psychologists and psychiatrists and probably does
            not really exist.

_____ 10. If not properly treated, neurosis can turn into
            psychosis.

SAMPLE TEST QUESTIONS   (Review)

1. According to the _____, people are judged as abnormal
    if their thinking, feelings, or behavior interferes with
    their ability to function with their own lives or within
    society.

    a. statistical standard
    b. subjective discomfort approach
    c. maladaptive functioning approach
    d. abuse approach

2. According to the _____ model, abnormal behaviors such as depression or schizophrenia are assumed to be mental illnesses.

    a. psychosocial
    b. sociocultural
    c. medical
    d. demonic possession

3. The DSM-IV contains

    a. descriptions of categories of disorders
    b. recommendations for treatment of disorders
    c. theories regarding the causes of disorders
    d. medical prescriptions for disorders

4. All of the following are classified as anxiety states in which anxiety cannot be prevented by avoidance except

    a. phobias
    b. generalized anxiety disorder
    c. panic disorder
    d. obsessive-compulsive disorder

5. Long-lasting anxiety that is not focused on any particular object or situation is referred to as

    a. phobia
    b. free-floating
    c. panic
    d. nervousness

6. You have a friend who has exaggerated fear of open spaces. He is exhibiting the symptoms of

    a. hydrophobia
    b. claustrophobia
    c. agoraphobia
    d. acrophobia

7. Repetitive, ritualistic behaviors such as handwashing, counting, or putting things in order that are associated with an anxiety state are called

    a. obsessions
    b. compulsions
    c. ruminations
    d. phobias

8. Rape or assault victims who continue to feel unpleasant emotional reactions would be diagnosed as having a(n)

   a. obsessive-compulsive disorder
   b. phobia
   c. generalized anxiety disorder
   d. posttraumatic stress disorder

9. Hallucinations and delusions are symptoms of

   a. mood disorders
   b. personality disorders
   c. anxiety disorders
   d. schizophrenia

10. Antipsychotic drugs can decrease the symptoms of schizophrenia by decreasing the activity of

    a. dopamine synapses
    b. serotonin synapses
    c. the frontal lobes
    d. the autonomic nervous system

11. Family studies have shown that when it comes to schizophrenia, children are more similar to their

    a. biological parents than their adoptive parents
    b. adoptive parents than their biological parents
    c. friends than their families
    d. grandparents than their biological parents

12. A major difference between major depressive disorder and bipolar disorder is that only in bipolar disorders do people have

    a. hallucinations or delusions
    b. depression
    c. a biochemical imbalance
    d. manic episodes

13. This has been offered as a possible explanation for depression.

    a. inadequate bonding
    b. insufficient sleep
    c. learned helplessness
    d. Vitamin E deficiency

14. When depression comes on as a function of time-of-year, this is referred to as

    a. seasonal affective disorder
    b. mood disorder
    c. schizophrenia
    d. learned helplessness

15. The category of dissociative disorders includes

    a. amnesia, fugue, multiple personality
    b. multiple personality, generalized anxiety, obsessive disorder
    c. psychogenic amnesia, mood disorder, multiple personality
    d. mood disorder, conversion disorder, obsessive disorder

16. Dissociative amnesia involves

    a. wandering off
    b. memory loss
    c. changes in identity
    d. extreme nervousness

17. Dissociative fugue involves

    a. wandering off
    b. memory loss
    c. changes in identity
    d. genetic disorders

18. Egocentrism is characterized by

    a. preoccupation with one's own concerns
    b. general dizziness
    c. extreme laziness
    d. preoccupation with watching television

19. At the time of the early Greeks, who coined the term hysteria, it was believed that childless women and women without sexual partners suffered from various physical disorders that could be traced to their _____.

    a. eating habits
    b. wandering uterus
    c. upbringing
    d. estrogen level

20. A friend of yours uses drugs. These interfere with his social and work activities. In fact, she often does not show up for social events and often calls in sick to work. Your friend may be exhibiting

    a. substance abuse
    b. substance dependence
    c. substance related disorder
    d. schizophrenia

ANSWERS

FILL-IN EXERCISES

1. medical model   2. psychosis   3. Phobias   4. obsessive-
compulsive   5. posttraumatic   6. dopamine   7. major
depressive disorder, bipolar disorder   8. learned helplessness
9. dependence   10. labeling

SAMPLE TEST QUESTIONS

1.	c	11.	a
2.	c	12.	d
3.	a	13.	c
4.	a	14.	a
5.	b	15.	a
6.	c	16.	b
7.	b	17.	a
8.	d	18.	a
9.	d	19.	b
10.	a	20.	a

CHAPTER 13: THERAPY

OUTLINE   (<u>S</u>urvey & <u>Q</u>uestion)

Use this outline when you survey the chapter, and enter your questions and comments in the space provided.

TOPIC	**NOTES**

I.   ESSENTIALS OF PSYCHOTHERAPY

II. PSYCHOANALYSIS

    A.   Goals and Methods of Freudian Psychoanalysis: Exploring the Unconscious

    B.   Evaluating Psychoanalysis: Two Major Criticisms

III. COGNITIVE THERAPIES

    A.   Rational-Emotive Therapy: Changing Irrational Beliefs

B. <u>Critical Thinking</u>:
   Logic and Ellis's
   Rational-Emotive Therapy

C. Cognitive-Behavior
   Therapy: Treating
   Depression

D. Evaluating Cognitive
   Therapy: What are the
   Keys to Its Success?

IV. HUMANISTIC THERAPIES

A. Client-Centered Therapy:
   Carl Rogers's Approach

B. Gestalt Therapy:
   Becoming "Whole"

C. Evaluating Humanistic
   Therapy: Does It Help?

V. BEHAVIOR THERAPIES

A. Classical Conditioning
   Techniques: Changing
   Associations

B. Operant Conditioning
   Techniques: Changing the
   Consequences of Behaviors

C. Modeling: Changing Behavior
   By Watching Others

D. Evaluating Behavior Therapy:
   Successes and Problems

VI. GROUP THERAPIES

A. Family Therapy:
   Helping Families Cope

B. Encounter Groups:
   Promoting Personal
   Growth

A.   Institutionalization:
     Treating Chronic and
     Serious Mental Disorders

B.   Choosing the Right Therapy
     and Therapist: Tips for the
     Consumer

C.   <u>Gender</u> <u>and</u> <u>Cultural</u>
     <u>Diversity</u>: Cultural
     Variations and the
     Special Needs of Women
     in Therapy

LEARNING OBJECTIVES   (<u>R</u>ecite & w<u>R</u>ite)

After reading Chapter 13, you should be able to:

1. Define <u>psychotherapy</u> and discuss the five common areas of
    concern for all psychotherapies.

2. Define <u>psychoanalysis</u> and discuss its major goals. Describe
    the four methods free association, dream interpretation,
    resistance, and transference and how these methods reveal
    clues about unconscious mental processes.

3. Discuss the two major criticisms of psychoanalysis and how psychoanalysis have responded to their critics.

4. Describe the major assumptions of cognitive therapy and explain the specifics of Ellis's rational-emotive therapy.

5. Explain how Beck's cognitive-behavior therapy is useful for treating depression.

6. Discuss the successes and limits of cognitive therapy.

7. Identify the basic assumptions of humantistic therapies and discuss Rogers's client-centered therapy, including his three important qualities of communication.

8. Describe Perl's Gestalt therapy and discuss how it differs from Rogers' client-centered therapy.

230

9. Define <u>behavior</u> <u>therapy</u> and identify its basic assumptions and goals. Discuss how classical conditioning, operant conditioning, and modeling are used to change behavior.

10. Discuss the successes of behavior therapy and its three major criticisms.

11. Describe the three major advantages of group therapy over individual therapy and discuss family therapy, encounter groups, and support groups.

12. Discuss the successes of group therapies and the special problem of "pop therapies."

13. Identify the basic assumptions of biomedical therapies and discuss the use of drug therapy, electroconvulsive therapy, and psychosurgery.

14. Discuss the controversy surrounding institutionalization, including involuntary commitment and deinstitutionalization.

15. Explain how to find and choose a therapist, including the differences between therapists in their professional training. Discuss research findings regarding the effectiveness of therapy.

16. Discuss the cultural universals and cultural differences in therapy and the special needs of women in therapy.

KEY TERMS   (Recite and wRite)

Upon completion of Chapter 13, you should be able to define the following terms.

Antianxiety Drugs: _____

_____

Antipsychotic Drugs: _____

_____

Autism: _____

_____

Aversion Therapy: _____

_____

Behavior Therapy: _____

_____

232

Biomedical Therapy: _____

_____

Catharsis: _____

_____

Client-Centered Therapy: _____

_____

Clinical Psychologists: _____

_____

Cognitive-Behavior Therapy: _____

_____

Cognitive Therapy: _____

_____

Cognitive Restructuring: _____

_____

Countertransference: _____

_____

Deinstitutionalization: _____

_____

Drug Therapy: _____

_____

Eclectic Approach: _____

_____

Electroconvulsive Therapy (ECT): _____

_____

Empathy: _____

_____

Encounter Groups: _____

_____

Family Therapy: _____

_____

Free Association: _____

_____

Genuineness: _____

_____

Gestalt Therapy: _____

_____

Hierarchy: _____

_____

Humanistic Therapy: _____

_____

Interpretation: _____

_____

Lobotomy: _____

_____

Modeling Therapy: _____

_____

234

Naikan Therapy: _____

_____

Psychiatrist: _____

_____

Psychoanalysis: _____

_____

Psychoanalyst: _____

_____

Psychosurgery: _____

_____

Psychotherapy: _____

_____

Rational-Emotive Therapy (RET): _____

_____

Resistance: _____

_____

Social Worker: _____

_____

Systematic Desensitization: _____

_____

Tardive Dyskinesia: _____

_____

Time Out: _____

_____

Token: _____

_____

Token Economy: _____

_____

Transference: _____

_____

Unconditional Positive Regard: _____

_____

FILL-IN EXERCISES   (<u>R</u>eview & w<u>R</u>ite)

Fill in the word or words that best fit in the spaces below.

1. _____ is a general term for the various methods of
    therapy that aim to improve psychological functioning and
    promote adjustment to life.

2. Sigmund Freud developed _____ to alter unconscious
    conflicts that have been _____ by ego defense mechanisms.

3. Albert Ellis's therapy, called _____, is an attempt to
    change the troubled person's belief system.

4. One of the most successful applications of Aaron Beck's
    cognitive-behavior therapy is in the treatment of _____.

5. Carl Rogers's therapy, called _____, focuses on
    encouraging healthy emotional experiences.

6. _____ changes associations through the classical conditioning technique of pairing deep relaxation with the visualization of a(n) _____ of anxiety-arousing images.

7. In sharp contrast to systematic desensitization, _____ therapy uses principles of classical conditioning to create anxiety rather than extinguish it.

8. _____ therapy involves watching and imitating appropriate models who demonstrate desirable behaviors.

9. The dramatic reduction in numbers of hospitalized mental patients is attributed to the use of _____.

10. A Japanese form of therapy that aims to help a person discover personal guilt and develop gratitude to others is referred to as _____ therapy.

APPLICATION (Recite)

Situation

One of the major problems of today's society is what to do with all of the homeless people. If you live in or have visited a large city, you have no doubt seen people sleeping on the sidewalks or just standing around.

Questions to Answer

1. With regard to the information you obtained in Chapter 16, what might be one of the reasons for homelessness?

2. Can psychologists do anything to help the homeless? Give examples.

3. Are there any methods you can mention that might reduce the rate of homelessness attributed to psychological reasons?

4. Can that proportion of homelessness attributed to psychological reasons ever be eliminated? What might be some steps in this direction?

CRITICAL THINKING EXERCISE (<u>R</u>ecite)

<u>Expressing Empathy</u>   (An Affective Skill)

According to Dr. Thomas Gordon, people who wish to express empathy must avoid asking questions or giving advice when it is more appropriate to explore the other person's emotional state. Instead, the technique of "active listening" he recommends uses open-ended statements that enable your partner to express feelings.   Three active listening techniques are:

   a.   repeat what was said as a statement rather than a question

   b.   slightly reword (or paraphrase) the statement

   c.   state the feeling you assumed was being expressed

Use either of the last two possibilities for each of the following (the first example has been completed for you so that you will get the idea):

1.   "I had the worst day of my life today at work."

<u>"Do you mean that everything you did at work today seemed to go</u>

<u>wrong?"</u>

2.   "I feel like a nobody--no one ever pays attention to me or seems to care about me."

_____

_____

3.   "You always seem to hurt my feelings."

_____

_____

SAMPLE TEST QUESTIONS   (Review)

1. The application of drugs and other medical procedures to correct a psychological problem or condition is

    a. psychotherapy
    b. biomedical therapy
    c. ECT
    d. cognitive restructuring

2. Catharsis is

    a. free-floating anxiety
    b. release of tensions and anxieties
    c. falling in love with the therapist
    d. a form of biological therapy

3. In psychoanalytic dream interpretation, the actual events of the dream are known as the _____ content.

    a. manifest
    b. latent
    c. subconscious
    d. transference

4. Free association and dream interpretation are psychoanalytic therapy techniques that are used to

    a. analyze intrapsychic conflicts
    b. keep unconscious conflicts out of awareness
    c. restructure the self-concept
    d. countercondition

5. In _____, mistaken beliefs or misconceptions are actively disputed.

    a. client-centered therapy
    b. psychoanalysis
    c. rational-emotive therapy
    d. systematic desensitization

6. According to the perspective of rational emotive therapy, a consequence such as depression or anxiety occurs as a result of a(n)

    a. activating experience
    b. stimulus event
    c. conditioning experience
    d. belief

7. A client-centered therapist emphasizes the importance of

    a. supporting the positive growth of the self-concept
    b. rewarding appropriate behaviors
    c. appropriate role models
    d. creating insight and catharsis

8. Sharing another person's inner experience is known as

    a. unconditional positive regard
    b. genuineness
    c. empathy
    d. sympathy

9. In Gestalt therapy, this is an exercise in which the therapist asks "what" questions.

    a. wholeness exercise
    b. awareness exercise
    c. empathy exercise
    d. closure exercise

10. _____ creates a hierarchy which is used to extinguish anxiety.

    a. Cognitive therapy
    b. Aversion therapy
    c. Systematic desensitization
    d. Psychoanalysis

11. You have an aunt who has been trying to stop smoking for a long time. She recently tried a treatment where she was given a brief electric shock whenever she lit up a cigarette. This smoking-control procedure is known as

    a. aversion therapy
    b. counterconditioning
    c. systematic desensitization
    d. behavior rehearsal

12. In behavior therapy, this use of negative punishment removes people from sources of rewards whenever they behave inappropiately.

    a. time out
    b. extinction
    c. modeling
    d. time in

13. This form of therapy treats the family as an unit, and members work together to resolve problems.

    a. aversion therapy
    b. family therapy
    c. encounter therapy
    d. parent-sibling therapy

14. Antianxiety drugs are also known as

    a. uppers
    b. "major tranquilizers"
    c. "minor tranquilizers"
    d. sympathetic drugs

15. Tardive dyskinesia is thought to be a side effect of treatment with _____ medication.

    a. mood-altering
    b. psychoactive
    c. antianxiety
    d. antipsychotic

16. This form of therapy involves physiological interventions to reduce symptoms associated with psychological disorders.

    a. ECT
    b. cognitive therapy
    c. mood therapy
    d. biomedical therapy

17. ECT is now used primarily in the treatment of

    a. depression
    b. anxiety
    c. phobias
    d. schizophrenia

18. The original form of psychosurgery developed by Egaz Moniz disconnected the _____ lobes from the midbrain structures where emotional experiences are relayed.

    a. occipital
    b. parietal
    c. temporal
    d. frontal

19. Your friend graduated from medical school and only sees patients with behavioral disorders. In all likelihood, she is a

    a. psychologist
    b. social worker
    c. psychiatrist
    d. marriage counselor

20. A(n) _____ therapist is most likely to use techniques from different theoretical orientations.

    a. humanistic
    b. psychoanalytic
    c. neo-Freudian
    d. eclectic

ANSWERS

<u>FILL-IN</u> <u>EXERCISES</u>

1. Psychotherapy   2. psychoanalysis, repressed
3. rational-emotive   4. depression   5. client-centered
6. Systematic desensitization, hierarchy   7. aversion
8. Modeling   9. drug therapy   10. Naikan

<u>SAMPLE</u> <u>TEST</u> <u>QUESTIONS</u>

1.	b	11.	a
2.	b	12.	a
3.	a	13.	b
4.	a	14.	c
5.	c	15.	d
6.	d	16.	d
7.	a	17.	a
8.	c	18.	d
9.	b	19.	c
10.	c	20.	d

CHAPTER 14: SOCIAL PSYCHOLOGY

OUTLINE   (<u>S</u>urvey & <u>Q</u>uestion)

Use this outline when you survey the chapter, and enter your
questions and comments in the space provided.

TOPIC   NOTES

I.   SOCIAL INFLUENCE

     A.   Conformity: Going
          Along With Others

     B.   Obedience: Going
          Along With a Command

     C.   <u>Critical</u> <u>Thinking</u>:
          Would You Have Followed
          Koresh or Jones?

II. GROUP PROCESSES

     A.   Group Membership:
          How It Affects the
          Individual

244

C. Loving: The Many
   Faces of Love

V. ATTITUDES

   A. Components of Attitudes:
      Cognitive, Affective, and
      Behavioral

   B. Cognitive Dissonance:
      How We Sometimes Change
      Our Own Attitude

   C. Persuasion: Direct
      Attempts at Attitude Change

VI. PREJUDICE AND DISCRIMINATION

   A. Sources of Prejudice and
      Discrimination: Five
      Major Factors

246

B. Gender and Cultural
    Diversity: The Price
    of Prejudice and Discrimination

C. Reducing Prejudice and
    Discrimination: Three
    Major Methods

VII. AGGRESSION

A. Internal Factors:
    Instinct and Biology

B. External Factors:
    Frustration, Social
    Learning, and Group
    Influence

C. Controlling or Eliminating
    Aggression: Can We Do It?

VIII. ALTRUISM

A. Why Do We Help?
   Biological and Psychological
   Explanations

B. Why Don't We Help?
   Diffusion of
   Responsibility

C. Increasing Altruism:
   How Can We Promote Helping?

LEARNING OBJECTIVES   (<u>R</u>ecite & w<u>R</u>ite)

Upon completion of Chapter 14, you should be able to:

1. Define <u>social psychology</u> and list the two major forms of
   social influence.

2. Define <u>conformity</u> and discuss Asch's famous study on
   conformity and explain the role of normative social
   influence, informational social influence, and reference
   groups.

3. Define <u>obedience</u> and discuss the major factors that
   influence it. Describe how destructive obedience can be
   reduced.

4. Define what is meant by a "group." Describe the two major ways that group membership affects individual behavior (i.e., roles and deindividuation).

5. Describe Zimbardo's prison study and explain how it demonstrates the power of roles on behavior.

6. Discuss how group polarization and groupthink affect decision making in groups.

7. Define <u>attribution</u> and discuss how consistency, consensus, and distinctiveness help us make accurate attributions.

8. Discuss two errors in attribution: the fundamental attribution error and the self-serving bias.

9. Explain the role of physical attractiveness, proximity, and similarity in interpersonal attraction and discuss cultural differences in perceptions of physical attractiveness.

10. Describe Rubin's distinction between liking and loving.

11. Compare and contrast romantic and companionate love. Discuss problems with romantic love.

12. Define <u>attitude</u> and describe the three basic components of all attitudes. Discuss why attitudes do not always match behaviors.

13. Define <u>cognitive dissonance</u> and describe the related experiment performed by Festinger and Carlsmith.

14. Discuss self-perception theory and how it differs from cognitive dissonance theory.

15. Define <u>persuasion</u> and describe how characteristics of the source, the message, and the audience influence persuasion.

16. Define <u>prejudice</u> and describe the three components of this attitude.

17. Identify how prejudice differs from discrimination.

18. Discuss the five major sources of prejudice and discrimination: learning, cognitive processes, individual personality needs, economic and political competition, and displaced aggression.

19. Discuss power inequality as a "cost" of prejudice.

20. Describe the three major methods for reducing prejudice: cooperation, superordinate goals, and increased contact.

21. Define <u>aggression</u> and discuss how instinct and biology have been used as explanations for aggressive behavior.

22. Discuss the three major external factors in aggression: frustration, social learning, and group influence.

23. Describe the three major approaches to controlling or eliminating aggression.

24. Define <u>altruism</u> and discuss the biological explanations for helping behaviors.

25. Discuss the two major psychological explanations for altruism: the egoistic model and the empathy-altruism hypothesis.

26. Explain why we sometimes don't help others and how we can promote helping behaviors.

KEY TERMS   (Recite and wRite)

Upon completion of Chapter 14, you should be able to define the following terms:

Aggression: _____

_____

Altruism: _____

_____

Attitude: _____

_____

Attribution: _____

_____

Authoritarian Personality: _____

_____

Blaming the Victim: _____

_____

Cognitive Dissonance Theory: _____

_____

252

Companionate Love: _____

_____

Conformity: _____

_____

Credibility: _____

_____

Deindividuation: _____

_____

Diffusion of Responsibility: _____

_____

Discrimination: _____

_____

Empathy-Altruism Hypothesis: _____

_____

Foot-in-the-Door Technique: _____

_____

Frustration-Aggression Hypothesis: _____

_____

Fundamental Attribution Error: _____

_____

Group: _____

_____

Group Polarization: _____

_____

Groupthink: _____
_____

Informational Social Influence: _____
_____

Ingroup Favoritism: _____
_____

Interpersonal Attraction: _____
_____

Need Compatibility: _____
_____

Need Complementarity: _____
_____

Negative State Relief: _____
_____

Norm: _____
_____

Normative Social Influence: _____
_____

Obedience: _____
_____

Outgroup Homogeneity Effect: _____
_____

Outgroup Negativity: _____
_____

Persuasion: _____
_____

Physical Attractiveness: _____
_____

Prejudice: _____
_____

Proximity: _____
_____

Reactance: _____
_____

Reference Groups: _____
_____

Role: _____
_____

Romantic Love: _____
_____

Saliency Bias: _____
_____

Self-Perception Theory: _____
_____

Self-Serving Bias: _____
_____

Similarity: _____

_____

Social Psychology: _____

_____

Stereotype: _____

_____

Superordinate Goal: _____

_____

FILL-IN EXERCISES

Fill in the word or words that best fit in the spaces below.

1. The two major types of social influence are _____ and
   _____.

2. _____ social influence results from individuals' need
   for belonging and group acceptance, whereas _____ social
   influence involves conforming out of a need for direction
   and a lack of alternatives.

3. _____ refers to the fact that after a group discussion,
   a member's preexisting and dominant tendencies or opinions
   will be reinforced and intensified.

4. When judging the causes of others' behavior, we tend to
   overestimate personality factors and underestimate social or
   situational factors, a bias known as _____.

5. _____ love seems to place heavy emphasis on mystery and
   fantasy, whereas _____ love seems to be based on mutual
   respect, trust, and friendship.

6. The three major components of all attitudes are the _____,
   the _____, and the _____.

7. The need for _____, or harmony between our attitudes, often leads us to change our attitudes when we experience _____ from noticing the mismatch.

8. Once people believe that they are no longer free to choose or to disagree with the persuader, they often increase their resistance to persuasion--a phenomenon termed _____.

9. According to the _____ hypothesis, aggression is always a consequence of frustration and frustration always leads to some form of aggression.

10. The major reason why Kitty Genovese's neighbors failed to respond to her cries for help was because of the _____ phenomenon.

APPLICATION   (<u>R</u>ecite)

<u>Situation</u>

You have never cheated on an exam. However, you are now enrolled in a course that is so difficult that no matter how much you study, you cannot seem to pass the exams. A group of students in the class has decided to cheat on the final exam, the exam that counts half of your total grade. In desperation, you agree to become a member of this group.

<u>Questions</u> <u>to</u> <u>Answer</u>

1. Describe some of the processes that are involved in your deciding to become a member of the cheating group.

2. What are the negative social consequences of joining this group?

3. What are the positive social consequences of joining this group?

4. What might be your own personal consequences for having joined this group?

CRITICAL THINKING EXERCISE   (Recite)

Applying Knowledge To New Situations   (A Behavioral Skill)

A critical thinker is often able to take an existing situation
and apply the knowledge acquired to new or future situations.
This type of analysis leads the critical thinker to interpret
events or situations in new, important ways. By being a critical
thinker, you will be able to apply the information learned about
prejudice in Chapter 14 to future events.

To increase your own awareness of the prejudices on your college
campus, ask a member of the opposite sex to be your partner in
the following exercise:

Visit both the male and female bathrooms (use your opposite sex
partner for the appropriate bathroom) of three separate buildings
on your college campus (e.g., the art department, the business
department, the psychology department). Record your observations
after each question.

1. Did you notice any graffiti directed at certain minority
    groups?

    _____

    _____

2. Was there a difference between the male and female
    prejudices (as expressed by the graffiti)?

    _____

    _____

3. Did you notice a difference in "graffiti prejudice" in the
    three buildings?

    _____

    _____

4. What does this say about the causes of and treatment for
    prejudice?

    _____

    _____

SAMPLE TEST QUESTIONS (Review)

1. The branch of psychology that studies how an individual's behavior (thoughts, feelings, and actions) is influenced by other people is

   a. sociology
   b. social psychology
   c. social behaviorism
   d. sociometry

2. Conforming to the typical behaviors of society out of a need for approval and acceptance is known as

   a. normative social influence
   b. informational social influence
   c. obedience
   d. reference group adherence

3. Waldo changes his behavior in response to the demands of his friends. He is exhibiting _____.

   a. conformity
   b. compliance
   c. obedience
   d. socialization

4. In Zimbardo's prison experiment, the majority of the subjects with the role of prisoner became

   a. combative
   b. defiant
   c. passive
   d. manic depressive

5. _____ seem(s) to be the most important factor(s) in deindividuation.

   a. Individual temperament and personality
   b. The authoritarian personality type
   c. Anonymity
   d. The size of the group

6. A group is strongly cohesive and its members have a shared desire for agreement; the members should be alert to the dangers of _____ in their decision making.

    a. group polarization
    b. groupthink
    c. brainstorming
    d. the "bandwagon" effect

7. Attribution

    a. explains how people use cognitive structures for exploring the world and explaining human behavior
    b. describes the principles we use in explaining what caused a behavior
    c. is usually unrelated to social perceptions
    d. is concerned with gambling behavior

8. People engage in the fundamental attribution error because

    a. it is easier to blame people than "things"
    b. people seem more conspicuously involved in the causes of things
    c. situations seem more difficult to control or change compared to people
    d. people miscalculate attributions

9. Research has consistently shown that physical attractiveness

    a. has little or no effect on interpersonal attraction
    b. is one of the most important factors in liking
    c. is associated with socioeconomic status
    d. is the same for all cultures

10. An intense feeling of attraction to another person characterized by high passion, obsessive thinking, and emotional fluctuation defines

    a. the arousal phase
    b. companionate love
    c. romantic love
    d. the sexual response cycle

11. Attitudes have three important components:

    a. the cognitive, the affective, and the behavioral
    b. the cognitive, the affective, and the consonant
    c. the consonant, the dissonant, and the compromise
    d. the actual, the fantasized, and the confabulated

12. Cognitive dissonance is associated with all <u>but</u> the following:

    a. a discrepancy between two or more inconsistent attitudes
    b. a discrepancy between attitudes and behavior
    c. psychological discomfort
    d. rationalization

13. When attempting to change personally valued and strongly held attitudes, the most important factor seems to be the

    a. physical attractiveness of the source
    b. amount of identification with the source
    c. degree of liking of the source
    d. credibility of the source

14. The learned predisposition to respond consistently in a positive or negative way to some person, object, or situation defines

    a. attitude
    b. belief
    c. prejudice
    d. stereotype

15. After attending a seminar on direct sales techniques, you remember a speech by someone who spoke very rapidly. After remembering this "fast talker," there is a reasonable likelihood that you would

    a. ignore everything he said
    b. be persuaded by what he said
    c. probably not remember what he said
    d. built counterarguments against what he said

16. A negative attitude directed toward some people because of their membership in a specific group is referred to as a(n)

    a. stereotype
    b. prejudice
    c. attitude
    d. discrimination

17. The prejudicial remark "They all look the same to me" is an example of

    a. ingroup favoritism
    b. outgroup negativity
    c. the outgroup homogeneity effect
    d. the ingroup heterogeneity effect

18. Any behavior that is intended to harm someone is referred to as

    a. aggression
    b. frustration
    c. prejudice
    d. discrimination

19. Altruism refers to actions designed to help others when

    a. there is no obvious benefit to oneself
    b. there is a benefit to the altruistic person
    c. they have previously helped you
    d. they are in a position to help you in the future

20. You are shopping in a mall and witness someone assaulting another individual. However, you do nothing to help the victim, figuring that others will help. You are exhibiting

    a. apathy
    b. prejudice
    c. diffusion of responsibility
    d. the outsider effect

ANSWERS

FILL-IN EXERCISES

1. conformity, obedience 2. Normative, informational
3. Group polarization 4. fundamental attribution error
5. Romantic, companionate 6. cognitive, affective,
behavioral 7. cognitive consistency, cognitive dissonance
8. reactance 9. frustration-aggression
10. diffusion of responsibility

SAMPLE TEST QUESTIONS

1.	b	11.	a
2.	a	12.	d
3.	c	13.	d
4.	c	14.	a
5.	c	15.	b
6.	b	16.	b
7.	b	17.	c
8.	a	18.	a
9.	b	19.	a
10.	c	20.	c